AUSTRALIAN
WAR DOGS

AUSTRALIAN WAR DOGS

The Story of Four-legged Diggers

Nigel Allsopp

This edition by New Holland Publishers in 2021
First published in 2012 by New Holland Publishers
Sydney • Auckland

Level 1, 178 Fox Valley Road, Wahroonga, NSW 2076 Australia
5/39 Woodside Ave Northcote, Auckland 0627 New Zealand

www.newhollandpublishers.com

A record of this book is held at the British Library and the
National Library of Australia.

ISBN 9781742579672

Group Managing Director: Fiona Schultz
Senior editor: Mary Trewby
Proofreader: Catherine Etteridge
Designer: Andrew Davies
Production Director: Arlene Gippert
Printed in China

10 9 8 7 6 5 4 3 2

Keep up with New Holland Publishers on Facebook
www.facebook.com/NewHollandPublishers

CONTENTS

Picture credits

The author would like to thank the following for supplying photographs:

Abbreviations: b = bottom; l = left; r = right; t = top; A = photos between pages 32 & 33; B = photos between pages 128 & 129

Australian Defence Force Media: A7b; A8b; B2b; B6t; B7tl; B8t. **Australian Defence Force Tracker & War Dog Association (ADFTWDA):** back cover right; A1; A2 (all); A3 (all); A4 (all); A5 (all). **Aaron Barnett:** B2t. **Dave Brown:** B6b. **John Cannon:** A7t. **Brett Charlton:** A6. **Sgt Mick Davis, 1st Joint Public Affairs Unit:** B8b. **ABIS Jo Dilorenzo:** B4–5. **Seamus Dohnerty:** A8t. **Jim Hoy:** A7br; B3b. **Cpl Rachel Ingram:** B7tr. **RAAF News:** B1t. **Vanessa Wallis:** B1br. **Shaun Ward:** front cover; B1bl, B7b. **WOFF Hungerford. RAAF:** back cover left; B3t

FOREWORD

I would like to point out up-front that I am not a trained dog handler. However, as the Officer Commanding Specialist Engineer Wing at the School of Military Engineering (which includes the Explosive Detection Dog Section), I am very aware of Military Dogs' contributions to the Australian Defence Force.

The capabilities Military Working Dogs bring to the Field Commander cannot be replicated by modern technology. There is nothing being developed anytime in the foreseeable future that will be able to cost-effectively and efficiently detect an offender or particular odour during day or night operations in the various environments we find ourselves operating. Military Working Dogs have served Australia well and have saved many Diggers' lives. Sadly, the ADF has had a handler and several dogs killed in action over recent years, losses that are keenly felt by the Defence community, but most keenly by that small, tight-knit group of soldiers that call themselves 'doggies'. Military Working Dogs, however, are still serving and protecting Australian personnel in environments from Afghanistan to East Timor, and will continue to play a vital role in future domestic security operations.

Australian War Dogs provides a fascinating insight to those who have not had the fortune to work with these exceptional animals. Attention to their service has gained much interest of late, but Military Working Dogs in the ADF have a long history that has gone relatively unnoticed by most. This book finally sheds some light on the role that they have played throughout this country's history.

Major J.A. Riley
Officer Commanding Specialist Engineer Wing
School of Military Engineering

WHY THE ANZACS SHOULD NEVER BE FORGOTTEN

ANZAC Day is important to every Australian, as it is a symbol of who we are as a people. We are a young country compared with many but our traditions forged in blood, honour, sacrifice and mateship define us as a nation.

We must continue to remember ANZAC Day each generation because it teaches each one of us what values Australia stands for. Those values are as important today as they were at the birth of our nation.

I am proud to live in this country, proud of generations of Australians who have sacrificed so much to enable me to live without fear and in freedom.

We must never forget first-generation Australians who sacrificed all at Anzac Cove alongside Australian-born sons. Whether we are of different faiths or cultures, we are all Australians first, all believing in its values and freedoms – that's why we are here.

When a protestor burns an Australian flag he should remind himself that he could only do so in a free country – a country that has sent its sons to war, some of whom return with that same flag draped over their coffins.

Lest we forget ...

Jessica-Lee Allsopp
Winner of RSL primary school competition

INTRODUCTION

In Australia we have always been a nation closely linked to the land and to animals. In our nation's early history the horse was perhaps the most influential animal to be introduced. It opened up Australia to settlers, allowing people to travel andexplorers to map the land and farm the outback. Soon to follow the horse was man's best friend, herding livestock and guarding settlements.

Alas we have not a great history in paying these animals which we owe so much back in kind. Hundreds of thousands of Whaler horses were drafted to serve the colours both for the Australian Army and other Commonwealth countries. All but one failed to return home. Australian servicemen were forced to shoot their equine mates or subject them to an even worse fate – leaving them in the hands of the local Egyptian population, who would work their own animals to death and think nothing of it.

Even one of Australia's outstanding animal icons, Murphy – aka Simpson's donkey – was left to an unknown fate on a far-off shore. The humble mule, the beast of burden, perhaps the real unsung hero of any military's logistics capability up to the end of World War II, has been neglected perhaps more than any other animal. So many mules were used by the services that no one knows the exact numbers. One thing is known however: we left them all overseas when war ended.

So we come to man's best friend, the four-legged digger, who is the subject of this book. During decades of global conflict, four-legged diggers have served alongside Australian troops. So what makes the canine useful in the art of war? A dog's qualities of loyalty, intelligence and devotion are highly valued in their role as pets, and these traits are also attractive to the armed forces. Among their many duties, our enlisted mates have helped carry messages through the trenches, laid telephone wire, and carried ammunition and medical equipment from place to place. A dog's keen sense of smell aided our soldiers in searching for and aiding the wounded and detecting mines, in a similar fashion to the bomb detector dogs of today.

Australian military forces enlisted the help of man's best friend during WWII when German Shepherds were given the task of watching over valuable military equipment. In Vietnam, the Australian Task Force included dogs in combat tracker teams. Their mission was to search the jungle for the enemy, and eleven four-legged diggers were left behind. There are many types of working dogs across the globe – but few are more critical to human life than those that sniff out explosives in Afghanistan. These dogs save the lives of Australian soldiers and civilians alike. Improvised Explosive Devices (IEDs) are the biggest threat to Australian soldiers in Afghanistan. They are often pre-positioned in or by a road in the hope that that coalition convoys will drive by. One of the vital assets in Australia's fight against IEDs is the Explosive Detection Dog (EDD). These dogs are specifically trained to sniff out explosives and, under the direction of a dog handler, provide an initial clearance of ground before human assets provide further clearance.

The following chapters explore the history of all Australian military working dogs throughout our history, their different roles within this period and what future dogs have in modern warfare.

Some specifics and names have been deliberately withheld due to ongoing activities and for security reasons.

Why such a book? Even though war dogs have served this country for more than a century, much of their efforts have escape public attention. This was highlighted to me during my research for the book when I realised there was a lack of dedicated memorials to animal sacrifices in war. Even today many returned service organisations (RSLs) do not include a plaque remembering animal deeds. The good news is this recognition is slowly on the increase, mainly thanks to the Australian Defence Force Tracker & War Dog Association (ADFTWDA), along with individual serving and ex-dog handlers who are ensuring that memorials are springing up throughout Australia. In fact I could not write any book on Australian war dogs without mentioning the ADFTWDA. In 2001, Leo Van De Kamp and Bob Bettany started the Australian Army Trackers & War Dogs Association, as it was known at that time. Its current name reflects the current recognition of today's military and service dogs in Australia. Throughout this book I mention various deeds such as the establishment and issue of War Dog Medals to serving Australian four-legged diggers. Within these pages you will also read how some of the association's committee members such as John Quane (secretary), Ian Hall (treasurer) and George Hulse (president) started their doggie careers and connections with war dogs and many years later are still driven to help current serving dog handlers. Today, the association's main quest is for the establishment of the Australian War Dog Association

Memorial to be constructed in the Wacol RSPCA Headquarters, Queensland.

The first Military Working Dogs (MWDs) to return to our shores from overseas deployments were three German Shepherds from the United Nations peacekeeping task force in Somalia in 1993. Maybe today's generation of servicemen will not accept a military dog serving in combat on operations overseas and being left in theatre or destroyed because quarantine restrictions prevent their return. Sadly, there have been far too many war dogs left to an unknown fate on enemy shores as we sailed home after the conflicts. Or, perhaps more cynically, there is an economic reason for bringing them home: an operational MWD can cost $50,000 once fully trained, with a shelf life of little more than half a dozen years of work so it's more cost effective not to discard them after each conflict.

Throughout this book I refer to dogs employed by the Australian Defence Force (ADF) as Military Working Dogs (MWD) and indeed in military circles they are mostly known by this. However this is for simplification. Within the armed services there are different roles for MWDs. In the Army Military Police, canines are known as Military Police Dogs (MPD). In the Army Engineers, specialist search dogs are called Explosive Detection Dogs (EDD). Within the RAAF, Military Working Dogs are often referred to as Service Police Dogs (SPD).

This book does not purport to be an official history but every effort has been made to provide the most accurate account possible, thanks to a wide variety of sources. The chapters about each service have been checked for accuracy by the respective current commanding officers; however, some gaps are inevitable as information has been lost over time. Like all institutions, both the RAAF and Army Military Working Dog units have had many people in their ranks over the years working tirelessly towards improving the standards, skills and welfare of dogs. In compiling this book, I have mentioned some individuals who have been kind enough to supply their stories. I must point out there are many others in the doggie trade who have developed procedures and helped give the book its present form. This is a history book, but I must further point out the great work undertaken by current serving members of the doggie trade who cannot for operational reasons be named. I thank these unsung heroes on behalf of the readers.

In the past, our use of animals with which we share this great nation has been in some cases less than honourable. Let's ensure we get it right for our canine mates. It is with pride that this book acknowledges all of our diggers, both two-legged and four-legged, who have and continue to serve Australia.

Photographs have been supplied by MWD handlers, both current and retired; by ADFTWDA, and by official government sources. Military working dog sections and images are reprinted with consent from the Australian Defence website.

A special thanks to respective dog handlers from military dog units from the Australian Defence Forces who supplied details and checked information for accuracy.

A GUIDE TO ACRONYMS USED IN THIS BOOK

ADF	Australian Defence Force
ADG	Airfield Defence Guard
AFP	Australian Federal Police
AK47	Soviet Bloc Rifle of 7.62 calibre
APC	Armoured Personnel Carrier
AQIS	Australian Quarantine and Inspection Service
ASLAV	Australian Light Armoured Vehicle
CER	Combat Engineer Regiment
EDD	Explosive Detection Dog
IED	Improvised explosive device
MDD	Mine Detection Dog
MEAO	Middle East Area of Operations
MP	Military Police
MPD	Military Police Dog
MRTF	Mentoring and Reconstruction Task Force
MTF	Mentoring Task Force

MWD	Military Working Dog
NDD	Narcotic Detection Dog
RAAF	Royal Australian Air Force
RAE	Royal Army Engineers
RAN	Royal Australian Navy
RAR	Royal Australian Regiments
RTF	Reconstruction Task Force
SECPOL	Security Police
SF	Special Forces
SME	School of Military Engineering
SOTG	Special Operations Task Group
TNI	Indonesian National Armed Forces

Sapper is a rank in the Army Engineers

Airman is a rank in the RAAF

Sergeant is a rank in the ADF

THE WAR ANIMAL'S PRAYER

Below is a prayer for the Remembrance of Animals at War. The first verse was written by an anonymous poet known as 'Sergeant 4486' from World War I, the second verse by Julie Taylor-Radcliffe.

The glamour gone, some scattered graves
and memories dim remain
With their old pals across a field, they'll never trek again
But yet there's nothing they regret as they await their call
For what was done or lost or won, they did their bit – that's all.

Now as silent as the guns have fallen
Their tired hearts resting, closed eyes of loving grace
I ask in your quiet thoughts of Honourable Remembrance
You allow them, the animals, to take their long awaited place.

Please in the silence of the hour spare some thought
for this forgotten Army.

1. HISTORY

WORLD WAR I

Following the German invasion of Belgium, on the morning of 4 August 1914 the British prime minister, Henry Asquith, announced a general mobilisation and demanded that Germany withdraw its forces from Belgium. With no reply forthcoming, at midnight on 4 August Britain declared war on Germany and sent out a telegram to all parts of the Empire, advising of the declaration of war. 'When the Empire is at war, so also is Australia,' Prime Minister Joseph Cook announced on 5 August. With that announcement, Australia was at war. The surge of patriotism in Australia was astounding as eager volunteers overwhelmed recruiting offices. So the First Australian Imperial Force (1st AIF) was born.

World War I saw the first large-scale employment of war dogs. Training was no longer more or less haphazard, but became organised and specialised. Records indicate that over 100,000 dogs were used during this conflict by all nations. War dog duties were many and varied and included such tasks as messenger, sentry, mine detection, ammunition and food carrier, mine dog, scout and guard, as well as casualty and ambulance duties.

Wireless was still being developed and signal cables were

often damaged during the fighting by heavy artillery fire. Dogs carrying messenger cylinders around their necks could run quickly from the forward trenches back to headquarters. These dogs faced the same dangers as the men on the battlefields, the same threats of bombardment and gas attack. Some were so frightened that they ran away, and enemy snipers shot many. The German units facing the Australians on the battlefield east of Villers-Bretonneux had no option but to communicate with their superiors via messenger dogs because of the Australian snipers. The Australians had earned a reputation for their aggressiveness as well as for the accuracy of their snipers and no-one understood this better than members of the German 1st Reserve Jaeger Battalion who were deployed in a series of small outposts opposite the Australians.

Although all armies used messenger dogs during WWI, it was not until the later stages of the war that the Australian Army carried out trials using dogs. Records indicate the Messenger Dog Sections were deployed into France. Number 3 Messenger Section was attached to the 4th Divisional Signal Company while operating with the 12th Brigade. The section comprised 16 men and 50 messenger dogs of various breeds. These dogs worked with fairly successful results, but were never solely relied on in sending messages. Three well-known dogs were War Dog 103 Nell, a Cross Setter; 102 Trick, a Collie; 101 Bullet, an Airedale. All three dogs were very efficient in message-carrying and saw service with the 2nd, 4th and 5th Australian divisions, also with divisions of the British 8th Corps (Imperial). 102 Trick was particularly efficient and was well-known by all brigades of the above-named divisions. He was specially mentioned by the signal officer of 2nd Division for good work at Rubimont, near Heilly.

The ADF has had a long association with animals and many

a Digger has adopted a battlefield companion. Even today, Royal Australian Regiments (RAR) have mascots such as eagles or sheep in their ranks. Australian forces, however, were slow to adopt animals in their order of battle such as MWDs or messenger pigeons. It appears Australian troops trusted animals far less to do a job than they did humans.

There were several reasons for this. Although some dogs used by Australian forces did sterling work, unfortunately on several occasions the same messenger dogs took off for hours on end without reporting to the other end of the message run. One reason was Aussie troops would feed their canine mates, which ruined the dogs' training because the two main ways to train a dog for this role is to use two dog handlers with whom the dog had rapport: it would run from one handler to the other and at the end the dog was fed. The more common method was a handler who had several dogs: he would dispatch a dog forward with an allied soldier who, when required, would place a message in a tube attached to the collar of the dog and then release him back to his master. As a reward, when the dog got back to his master he would be fed. Food as the reward was both the main key and problem.

This lure could cross boundaries, as Australian forces found during WWI when a German messenger dog, a Doberman called Roff, was tempted to cross the trenches outside Villers-Bretonneux by the prospect of some Aussie tucker. Private Rowan managed to coax the dog to come forward with some food and the dog showed little aggression. Private Rowan was subsequently too busy to worry much about the dog and it escaped again. However, this German dog seems to have taken a shine to the Australian troops and he was again captured by Captain Robert McKillop, MC, who was the commanding officer of D Company.

On 3 May 1918, Roff officially became a 'prisoner'. He was immediately renamed 'Digger' and made the 13th Battalion mascot. On 6 May 1918 the commanding officer of the 13th Battalion, AIF, Colonel Douglas Marks, DSO, MC, wrote to the Australian War Records Section advising that three days earlier his battalion had captured a German message dog at Villers-Bretonneux. Digger's capture became well known and even General John Monash mentioned the dog in a letter to a young relative. The dog was eventually passed to the 13th Battalion Quartermaster Store. Members of the battalion made him a dogcart and harness to carry supplies around the camp. He was good at it for a while, and as the men moved forward with the battle, he went with them. But Digger's behaviour slowly deteriorated to such an extent that he became too savage to retain as a unit mascot. It was arranged for him to be sent to Bitterne Manor Farm Quarantine Kennels at Southampton on 19 September 1918. There he stayed. When the war ended and the Australian units commenced their slow repatriation home, it appears that Roff was forgotten, as no-one seemed to want to take responsibility for shipping him to Australia. Digger's health started to decline after he had been in quarantine for 12 months and on 15 October 1919 he died. Digger was skinned, stuffed and mounted and shipped to Australia for the Australian War Museum where he remains today.

WORLD WAR II

German aggression, this time against Poland, led the British prime minister Neville Chamberlain to declare war against its old adversary on 3 September 1939. Prime Minister Robert Menzies announced to the Australian nation that, '... as a result, Australia is also at war.' WWII was to last almost six years, again at a huge cost in human lives. Total loss of life for all combatants on both sides reached almost 25 million, with civilian losses exceeding 31 million. Germany surrendered unconditionally on 7 May 1945, but it took a further three months for the war in the Pacific to come to an end on 14 August 1945. The most devastating conflict in the history of the world had finally ended. It was just as devastating for the animals that served the colours. Even in this mechanised war, tens of thousands of horses died and canine four-legged diggers also paid the ultimate sacrifice.

Most nations had done little to maintain a war dog capability following the end of WWI. Germany, however, had continued to train dogs on a large scale between the world wars. At the outbreak of WWII, it had an army of some 200,000 trained dogs. All but a few would perish during the war.

Many thought that the end of WWI, also known as the Great War, would signal the end of messenger dogs because new radio technology would resolve the previous problems of battlefield communication. However, in the jungles of the Pacific Islands during WWII, messenger dogs again would be called upon to provide this service.

At the start of WWII, the Australian Army had no war dog capability. It was through information received on the training and development of military dogs in the United Kingdom and the United States of America that Australia commenced its own war dog training program. While details are incomplete, records indicate that in 1942 the Australian Army had developed a program to train general service dogs in scouting, early detection and installation protection.

It would appear that the US Army Quartermaster Corps provided the scout dogs used by the Australian Army during the New Guinea campaigns. It is possible that at least one dog named 'Gyp', a guard dog, was trained in Australia and may have accompanied the 214th Pioneer Battalion, 1st Beach Landing Group, to New Guinea in November 1944. Little is known of this dog, its origin or where it was trained. It is unlikely, however, that only one dog would have been sent in isolation and it can be assumed that a number of other guard dogs were also sent abroad at that time.

A special training depot in Lowanna, New South Wales, was raised in 1943 as the First Army Experimental Dog Training Unit for dog handlers with their dogs. In May 1943 this unit consisted of 17 trained soldiers, each with two trained dogs. The dogs had been donated to the Australian Army after publicity in Sydney newspapers. Although a variety of breeds were used, the German Shepherd predominated.

Experiments were carried out on the training and use of dogs during war for:

- carrying messages
- scouting and guarding
- sniper hunting.

On 19 May, the unit consisting of 12 trained handlers and 24 war dogs under command of Captain Bamford, departed Sydney for Canungra, a military camp in Queensland. Records fail to indicate what transpired or whether the training was successful. However, a memo from the Australian commander-in-chief on 3 November 1943 advised that dogs were not to be employed in the Australian Army. This certainly suggests that the Canungra training trials had failed to convince the military hierarchy of the potential value that could be gained from the deployment of war dogs. It is interesting to note that while official Australian Army policy quashed the use of war dogs within the Army, the US Army was still providing Australian units serving in New Guinea with dogs. One such dog was 'Sandy', which was trained by the United States Dog Detachment for the 2/27th Australian Infantry Battalion. Sandy worked with two Australian handlers, Privates J.G. Worchester and J.R. Sutton. The dog was trained to carry messages from one location to another, travelling from one handler to another. Sandy was one of many scout and messenger dogs trained by the USA and attached to the Australian Army during the New Guinea campaign. Little is known about the actual number of American-trained dogs that was deployed with the Australians.

In March 1944 a report was received from the Australian Military Mission in Washington DC on the use of dogs for detection of minefields. The Australian Army seems to have warmed to the idea and as no-one in Australia had any expertise in this area of war dog deployment, a request was put to the British Ministry of Defence for the use of a dog instructor. On 8 July 1944 the Australian commander-in-chief was advised by the War Office in London that, 'It is not possible to send a first class dog instructor,'and suggested that 'Australia send possible trainers to a UK war dog school.' As a result, just six months after the commander-in-chief had cancelled war dog training in the Australian Army, war dogs were again on the agenda.

In September 1944 it was decided to send Captain Harry Bamford and Warrant Officer First Class Michael Busst to Britain to attend a three-month course at the War Dog Training Centre. After completing this training in early February 1945, Captain Bamford and Warrant Officer Busst visited the USA on their way back to Australia and were attached to the US War Dog School at Fort Robinson, Nebraska. It is interesting to note that war dog training was being carried out by the US Quartermaster Corp on an extensive scale but the training of dogs for mine detection had been discontinued. The American focus was on scout and messenger dog training, areas that had been rejected earlier by the Australian Army. The US Army rationale for rejecting mine detection training was based on tests conducted under field conditions in theatres of operation; these indicated that, 'while dogs could find a good percentage of buried mines, the percentage was not high enough to justify the use of dogs as a substitute for more efficient mechanical devices.'

While in Britain, Captain Bamford submitted a report recommending the establishment of an Australian war dog training school. He recommended that a training school be established in Australia as a complete unit, isolated from other military establishments, in order to avoid interference in the training and handling of dogs. The school should be located close to a capital city, Sydney preferably because of the proximity of Rosemount Veterinary Hospital and the School of Military Engineering. Dogs should be procured by public appeal, as was the case in Britain He further recommended the creation of a war dog platoon, which should be manned by one officer and 22 other ranks and 30 dogs.

The war dog platoon was subsequently raised on Australia's War Establishment and included one officer with a headquarters and two dog-handling sections, a total of 23 all ranks plus 36 war dogs. Little is known about the 1 Australian Dog Platoon (RAE), although it is clear from records that soldiers were posted to the unit, which was eventually disbanded on 7 August 1945. After returning to Australia, Captain Bamford submitted his report, which outlined both the advantages and disadvantages involved with the use of mine-detecting dogs. The result was not clear-cut and considerable discussion ensued on whether this training should go ahead. On 30 April 1945, the military secretary, in a letter to the engineer-in-chief, wrote that Captain Bamford's report seemed to suggest that the disadvantages of using mine-detecting dogs outweighed the advantages and sought further advice.

On 12 May 1945 in a Minute to the director of military training, the engineer-in-chief outlined the pros and cons of war dog training and concluded that, 'It is considered that it would be uneconomical in manpower to train a Dog Platoon for the areas in which the Australian Forces are at present fighting, or likely to fight. It is therefore recommended that no further action be taken to train a Dog Platoon.' Three days later the engineer-in-chief recommended that the 1 Australian Dog Platoon be struck off the Order of Battle and that Royal Australian Engineer (RAE) units, in accordance with current priorities, absorb the existing personnel.

KOREA

The crisis in Korea originated in the closing phases of WWII. Control of the Korean peninsula, formerly occupied by Japan, was entrusted to the Allies and the Soviet Union, to be divided between them at the 38th parallel. Over the course of the next few years tensions between the two zones, each under a different regime, escalated to the point where two hostile armies were building up along the border. On 25 June 1950 the North Korean Army finally crossed into the southern zone and advanced towards the capital, Seoul. Twenty-one nations, including Australia, responded to a United Nations call by providing troops, ships, aircraft and medical teams.

The order cancelling the training of war dogs in the Australian Army was relatively short lived: it seems that the Allies had finally learnt their lesson in regard to war dog training following the end of WWII. With the outbreak of the Korean War, both the US and British forces had a considerable war dog capability, which had not only been retained after World War II but had been actively enhanced.

The Americans as well as the British Army had been using dogs for a long time and they had proved invaluable. Although no accurate figures are available, the US used about 1500 dogs during the Korean War and claimed that the scout dogs used in Korea actually reduced the casualty rate by 65 per cent. In fact one such dog, 'York', received a presidential citation for leading 148 combat missions and not losing a single man due to enemy fire. Australia, however, had not developed such a capability. Although the Australian battalions used dogs in Korea with good results, the Australian Army as an entity began using patrol and tracker dogs as far back as the Korean War, the Malayan Emergency, and in Borneo. Members of the British Army's RAVC and SAS units then conducted dog training.

In Korea the British Royal Engineers trained Australian servicemen with dogs. One of these dogs was called Bruce and, unlike other patrol dogs, he was not the standard tan-and-black German shepherd. Bruce was snowy white. It was good camouflage in winter, when snow lay thick on the Korean hills. But in summer he couldn't avoid being seen on patrol. Dyeing Bruce with coffee solved this problem. The Royal Engineers would make a good strong brew, let it cool, and then rub the coffee into his coat. Once dry, they'd rub in more cold coffee, until Bruce was as brown as the other shepherds.

It was not until almost the end of the conflict that Australia finally recognised the need for dog-handling expertise to be integral to a battalion's capability. In late May 1953 a number of Australian soldiers were selected to attend a dog handler's course. Due to the departure of the Royal Engineers dog handlers who had completed their 12-month tour, and with the ceasefire imminent, new handlers were trained from within the Division for the remainder of the war. Consequently, a soldier from each battalion of the Commonwealth Division was selected to undertake the standard Royal Engineers dog handler's course, using the dogs that the departing Royal Engineers handlers had left behind.

The diggers who completed this training course as patrol dog handlers in Korea were the pioneers of what would be a new development in Australian infantry methods. The four Australian soldiers selected were Privates George Gray and Don Donaldson, both of the 2nd Battalion, Royal Australian Regiment (2 RAR), Lance Abbott from the 3rd Battalion RAR (3 RAR) and Bernard 'Blue' Mosch from the 1st Battalion RAR. All had a natural talent for working with animals. The training course was conducted by the War Dog Troop of the First British Commonwealth Division at 64 Field Park Squadron Royal Engineers, just south of the demilitarised zone. The War Dog Troop was originally responsible for the training of 14 dogs in total (two were killed during the war), consisting of infantry patrol dogs, guard dogs, mine dogs and Red Cross dogs.

The original commander of the Dog Troop was Sergeant Ken Bailey, a Royal Engineers sergeant of some fame who had trained the inaugural London police dog handlers. Sergeant Bailey's role was not simply an administrative one as he also personally ran the dog handler's course. His training expertise was highly regarded, which possibly accounts for his position in command at the rank of sergeant. Upon his departure Lieutenant Peter Goss from the 3rd Battalion RAR, the only Australian officer to have filled such a position in Korea, replaced him. The senior non-commissioned officer during this period responsible for the actual training was Staff Sergeant Glen 'Taffy' Shaw, a qualified and experienced dog trainer from the Royal Army Veterinary Corps of the British Army. Following the successful completion of the course, Staff Sergeant Shaw, who had been training dogs and dog handlers for the British Army for the previous eight years, said that the secret of success was patience, tact, and understanding:

Australians appear to have a remarkable aptitude for this job. They are excellent pupils, they are dog lovers, and the dogs respond to them very well. I have trained British, Germans, Poles, Yugoslavs, Egyptians, and soldiers of many other races, but these four men are about the best pupils I have ever had. Maybe it is because the digger is a natural-born patrol soldier, and they seem to get on better with dogs than anyone else. I wish I had more of them.

Patrol dog training was the only course taken by the Australians. It took the first week for each man to get to know the dog he had to handle. Although the War Dog Troop used a number of breeds for various purposes, in the main the patrol dogs were German Shepherds of superior intelligence, especially trained to merely indicate the presence of enemy. Before training could begin, the handler had first to win the confidence and respect of the dog. He was then taught how to care for the dog, to feed, groom and give veterinary first aid, how to handle the animal and work the dog on the particular task required. Training with patrol dogs also involved long and arduous work, day and night, climbing steep mountains, then sliding down steeper slopes into winding valleys under battle patrol conditions. All the time the handler had to concentrate on developing coordination between himself and his dog, coordination that would stand in good stead whenever the time came that they would have to work as a team in actual warfare. The Australian quartet became so adept at handling the dogs that in their final tests they were able to detect ambushes set for them on their patrols at distances of up to 500 yards (about 460 metres).

On the Korean battlefield few Australian troops seriously regarded the dogs as allies that could help save lives. They might have accepted the dogs more quickly if they'd had worked with

'Eros', a genuine German Shepherd from Germany trained as a military guard dog. The dog was a real killer and had a mean streak in him – today he would be referred to as a 'land shark'. The old school of military dogs used to aggressively patrol bases for intruders. Another reason for him feeling angry may have been the fact that he had been injured on patrol at the frontline. After an enemy grenade exploded near him, Eros lost part of two toes on his right paw, and a small piece of shrapnel lodged in his back. The vets operated successfully, but for a while Eros was among the walking wounded. Once trained as a patrol dog, Eros could sense any hostile force. He'd sit and point with his head directly at an ambush.

The soldiers of the First Commonwealth Division War Dog Troop had room for sentiment. Just prior to the ceasefire, one of the best dogs in the kennel, 'Killer', died when the Chinese ambushed a patrol from the Royal Canadian Regiment, killing two men and wounding another. This was the only time a patrol led by a dog was ambushed during the Korean campaign, this being the fault of a soldier who refused to accept the animal's signal. The dog's handler, Sapper Les Wain of Yorkshire, carried Killer's body out of the valley and took it back to the kennels, where it was buried. A cross inscribed 'Killer KIA 12/7/1953' marked the head of the grave and a large headstone featuring a dog, picked out in whitened stones, was constructed.

Beside Killer was buried 'Teddy', a mine dog and veteran of WWII. Teddy was a qualified paratrooper, having successfully parachuted into Germany with the Royal Engineers. He died from snakebite in a Korean minefield. Every day, while the unit was stationed there, one of the handlers placed bunches of flowers on both Killer's and Teddy's graves. Killer and Teddy were the only War Dog Troop canine casualties.

When the ceasefire came into effect on 27 July 1953, the four Australians who had completed the Royal Engineers dog handler's course served out the remainder of their tour of duty with the War Dog Troop, leading night patrols along the demarcation zone. They returned to Australia in 1954. Both George Gray and Lance Abbott continuing as dog handlers in the Australian Army. Lieutenant (Lt) Peter Goss and Corporal George Gray were later to soldier on with 2 RAR in Malaya.

The War Dog Troop of the First British Commonwealth Division in Korea was eventually disbanded. It is thought that the dogs may have completed their service career in Korea or perhaps Malaya.

Captain John M Hutcheson was born in 1927 at Townsville, Queensland, and entered Duntroon on 24 February 1945, graduating into the Royal Australian Engineers (RAE) with the rank of lieutenant. In 1952, he was posted to Japan to the British Commonwealth Forces – Korea (BCFK). While in Japan, he was re-posted to 3 RAR as Assault Pioneer Platoon Commander.

Caption Hutcheson had the job of locating and plotting minefields onto maps. He also handled a dog himself in this area. For this work, John was awarded a personal Military Cross. It is noteworthy that John must be the only person in military history who handled a war dog on operations at the rank of captain and with a MC.

During one patrol into no-man's land a British lance corporal attached to 3 RAR from the King's Regiment was killed. John had to go to the patrol's aid to bring them back through a minefield. Alas, the British soldier had to be left behind that night but the following night John set out again with a MWD to try and locate him. In John's own words:

I was given a mine-detecting dog and escorted by the same diggers who were attacked the night previously. I believe that these diggers were not too keen to do this patrol and they appeared a bit nervous to me. I led the patrol out with the dog on a long lead. We traversed the minefield and out into no-man's land, but then the dog caught the scent of dead and wounded Chinese soldiers who had been dragged away from the battle site toward Hill 75 (Matthew). These dead and wounded Chinese soldiers had been dragged by their mates to the Samichon River and then back into their own lines. The dog was following the drag marks and taking me straight toward the Chinese positions. The dog was a German Shepherd with good ability to detect mines and explosives and also track humans, particularly Chinese or North Koreans. However, the escort team were showing signs of not wanting to continue, so I called the dog off the search and we returned to our own lines. I did not locate the dead Lance Corporal. He was found and brought back the following day by another patrol.

Upon his return to Australia, John was promoted to major and became the Officer Commanding OC of Field Engineer Wing (FEW) at the Sydney School of Military Engineering (SME). It was decided that dogs were useful for mine detection, tracker work and guard duties and so, in 1953, the sappers at SME built dog kennels. John was the first OC FEW to have a mine dog section as a part of his command, and he recruited the initial handlers and dogs. Some dogs were purchased and others were donated to SME. A training program, which followed the British Army system, was introduced, and mine and guard dog training began in earnest. Some of the handlers had Korean experience, but many were yet to be tested on the battlefield known as the

'Malayan Emergency'in Malaya against the Communist terrorists. As Korea drew to a ceasefire, the Malayan Emergency (1948–60) gave a new sense of urgency to the dog section at SME.

Some Australian troops may have scoffed at the dogs, but the authorities were taking notice. As the war in Korea ended, the handlers who'd trained with the Royal Engineers were posted to a new war dog course at SME in Sydney: the first time that Australian working dogs would be trained in modern battle skills. It took a while for the ADF to get their heads around using living animals – our dogs were classified as 'engineer stores' and not war dogs. In transit or on war scales, there was never a requirement for 'engineer stores' to be fed, watered, groomed, toileted, fleaed, exercised, housed or trained, and sometimes the dogs suffered as a result of this – that is, until the handlers either threatened, coerced or 'found' suitable amenities for their dogs. The kennel master at this time was Corporal George Gray and John Hutcheson recognised his corporal as being the most appropriate trainer of the dogs. Corporal Gray was a very experienced dog trainer and handler in Korea and had received formal training in dog handling and training from the British Army's Royal Engineers. Corporal (later Sergeant) George Gray was a wonderful dog trainer who made a big impact on dog training in Malaya during the emergency. Sapper Lance Abbott arrived at SME in 1953 after serving with dogs in Korea.

With the spread of communism becoming a major threat in Malaya, and in anticipation of Australia's military involvement, the emphasis of the Mine Dog Section at SME was readjusted to incorporate both the training of infantry patrol dogs and tracking dogs. Each dog was selected for training in either patrol or tracking, but not both.

The patrol dogs were taught to work off lead and were deployed forward of the infantry unit, scouting the area ahead. They were taught to 'point' when an enemy presence was detected. It was only at night that these dogs were deployed in a harness because of the need for the handler to be close enough to detect a 'point'. Dogs were trained to recognise that when a short lead was placed on their collar their work was finished.

Tracker dogs were taught to follow the scent left by a fleeing quarry and to track the scent pattern, which automatically develops when a person or persons move through an area. These dogs always worked on harness and, depending on their ability, could detect the presence of their quarry from quite some distance away. As with patrol dogs, they recognised that their work was completed when the harness was removed.

Initially SME had gained their dogs from the RSPCA, taking any breed. However, many of these dogs proved unsuitable. Now, faced with the large training program for dogs and handlers, SME sought, and was given permission, to purchase its Labradors and German Shepherds.

Because of the cost involved, a stringent set of criteria was developed to ensure that only the most suitable dogs were purchased and every effort was made to identify suitable handlers for training. SME also began a breeding program. Because it was considered that future operations would involve jungle warfare, which might necessitate airborne insertion, it was decided that both handlers and their dogs should be parachute-qualified. Handlers and their dogs were sent to Williamtown in NSW to undergo parachute training and a harness was developed for the dogs. However, training was cancelled for the dogs when the Army was made aware by the RSPCA of the potential danger of trunk rotation, with possible spinal injury during a parachute descent.

By the end of 1954, preparation and training for deployment to Malaya was under full swing under the expert eye of Corporal George Gray, although it would not be until late 1955 that the first infantry troops would be deployed. This first contingent contained six dogs and their handlers. Although continuing in their mine dog role, SME would not provide any further dogs or handlers throughout the Malayan campaign. The Mine Dog Section continued its training role until 1959 when the unit was disbanded. It was again re-established at SME in 1969.

MALAYA

By the end of 1954, preparation and training for deployment to Malaya was in full swing under the expert eye of Crpl George Gray. Only a matter of weeks before they were due to embark from Brisbane, George and his team were advised of imminent deployment on active duty with the 2nd Battalion based at Enoggera in Brisbane.

A hectic period of preparation followed to ensure that all was in readiness for departure. Travelling from the SME by truck, the team and their dogs arrived at Enoggera Barracks to find that the battalion was ready to commence embarkation. After a final parade through the city with the battalion, they boarded the MV *Georgic*. With the ship's siren echoing three times across Moreton Bay, the 27,000-ton liner departed Brisbane on 8 October 1955. The ship docked at Penang Island on 20 October and the battalion was transported by road to Minden Barracks, located in foothills on the eastern side of the island. Although Minden Barracks was to be the nominal home of 2 RAR while it was in Malaya, due to operational demands the battalion was to spend very little time there.

When 2 RAR arrived in Malaya, the Australian Government

had not yet approved its participation in Malayan operations. As a result, the battalion did not start operations until January 1956. However, those three months were well spent acclimatising and training on Penang Island. The first anti-terrorist patrol operation was conducted in the Bongsu Forest Reserve in South Kedah. Operation Duece involved search and security activities and was typical of operations carried out by the battalion during its deployment in Malaya. These intense, lengthy patrols involved tracking the Communists through the jungle. The work was tiring, demanding and often frustrating, as there was little or no result. They found themselves seeking an elusive enemy, who struck without warning and then retreated into his jungle sanctuaries, avoiding contact with security forces. What was required to catch this fleeting enemy was the ability to follow his trails after detecting his presence by using the specially trained tracker teams and attaching native trackers (Iban people, or 'Sea Dyaks', from Sarawak) to rifle platoons.

The Australian battalion in Malaya was organised on a structure similar to the British and New Zealand battalions, which also served in 28 Commonwealth Independent Infantry Brigade. It had four rifle companies, each of three rifle platoons. There was also had a support company; this included an anti-tank platoon, which for its counter-insurgency missions during the Emergency, had been organised as a tracker platoon, usually with two teams each with tracker dogs and the attached Iban visual trackers.

Some successes were recorded using the dogs. During an operation, a dog which had accompanied a patrol commanded by Lieutenant Harry Smith from C Company in the Sungai Siput area, 'pointed' to an area ahead in the undergrowth. Sweeping through the area, Lieutenant Smith spotted a terrorist who was about to throw a hand grenade at the Australian patrol. In the ensuing contact, the terrorist was killed.

This is just one example of the effectiveness of war dogs. The dog involved in this action was 'Lauder', whose handler was Private Phil 'Sleepy' Daniel. Another member of this patrol was Private George Mansford, later to become brigadier and founder of the Baffle School in Tully, North Queensland. Many years later Lieutenant Harry Smith was to become Officer Commanding (OC) of Delta Company 6 RAR at the famous battle of Long Tan.

In another operation, a Communist terrorist (CT) ambush resulted in the killing of a young Australian planter and four special constables, once again in the Sungai Siput area. It was considered that a large group of enemy was involved in this action. It was decided to deploy tracker dogs, with a patrol from B Company to follow up and Privates C.D. (Honk) Crook with tracker dog 'Tex' and Phil Daniel with 'Lauder' were allocated the task. The CTs split into small groups and were scattering animal blood to confuse the trail. As a result, by last light, the patrol was unable to confirm whether the dogs were still on the track of the main body of the enemy group. That evening Private Daniel and 'Lauder' were redeployed with another patrol to search a different area.

The battalion's war dogs were well looked after. The British Army had full-time veterinarians of the Royal Army Veterinary Corps based at Seremban to provide professional care for the animals. Special kennels, with a fenced run, were constructed for the four dogs, far away from the soldiers' dining facilities. Unfortunately, the sighting was still close to the area where the 'Magnolia Man', a popular purveyor of Magnolia ice-creams, fruit juice and milk products, plied his wares at weekends. The soulful eyes of the dogs worked their magic on the troops, and eventually the vet ordered the overweight dogs onto a special exercise and ice-cream-free diet regime. One of the dogs, 'Gunnar', was an accomplished climber and escapologist. During an Officers' Mess barbecue, he was observed raiding the piles of sausages and steaks placed next to the barbecue pit by the Officers' Mess chef, Joe Dvoracsek, in readiness for the meal. The following Monday, the open run was topped with a wire mesh roof.

With the passage of time, the Australian Infantry took over responsibility of training tracker dogs and the Royal Australian Air Force (RAAF) took over the training of guard dogs. The call for explosive detection dogs and mine dogs diminished with the cessation of the Malayan Emergency, and so the Mine Dog Section at SME was terminated in 1959.

Corporal Arthur Eather was a rifleman with C Company (C Coy) 1 RAR when in September 1959, 1 RAR embarked for a tour of duty in northern Malaya. Shortly after arrival in the C Coy patrol base, a call for volunteers to become trained as trackers saw Arthur step forward for this training. In early 1960, he was sent to the British Army Battle School at Kota Tinggi in the southern state of Johore (next to Singapore). During this training Arthur was teamed up with three infantry patrol scout dogs named Wince, Rolfe and Thrush. The British Army delivered the training and the Australian diggers on that course were held in readiness for callout by helicopter in support of 1 RAR at short notice. These soldiers were now part of Support Company (Spt Coy) 1 RAR. After a successful tour Arthur returned to Australia in 1965 where he was in the Assault Pioneer Platoon because there was no tracker element in 1 RAR.

Arthur developed stomach ulcers and after treatment at the Concord Repatriation Hospital in Sydney, he was declared unfit for combat duty. This meant a posting out of 1 RAR and he was sent to the Transport Platoon of the Infantry Centre at Ingleburn and promoted to lance corporal. In 1966, he was approached by Lieutenant Barry French and Warrant Officer 2nd Class 'Blue' Carter to bring his Malaya tracker skills into a new wing being formed at the Infantry Centre called 'The Tracking Wing'. He accepted a role as an instructor and was promoted to corporal.

In May 1966, Private Norm Cameron arrived at the Tracking Wing and began his dog handler training under Arthur's direction. Although Barry was responsible for the overall management of the Wing and Blue trained the visual trackers, Arthur trained the dogs and handlers, using his experience in Malaya as his background. When Norm arrived in the Tracking Wing he found that Arthur was training up to 20 dogs and handlers in the bush. Arthur spent many weeks on end in the training areas around Ingleburn, Holsworthy and Bulli in NSW. He was an exacting taskmaster and watched every one of his dogs and trainee dog handlers with an eagle eye. His de-briefings were delivered in a no-frills manner and he made sure that his training experiences in the bush presented his trainees with as many and varied combat situations as he could muster. After any criticism of a trainee dog handler, Arthur would listen to the trainee's explanation, if any, and discuss it until the trainee was satisfied that there was nothing more to say about his performance. Arthur's weekly meetings with Barry and Blue always focused on positives for his diggers, but he was keenly aware that only the best would stay alive in a combat zone. Consequently, there were diggers and dogs who were just not suited for tracking work in the 'two-way rifle range'. The failure rate for the dogs was high, with about one dog in 20 being accepted as a MWD. His trainees regarded Arthur as a father-figure. Norm Cameron describes him as:

… a fair, thorough and highly regarded instructor who worked tirelessly to improve the conditions, kennels, veterinary care and equipment provided to tracker dogs and their handlers. As trainee dog handlers we could trust Arthur to look after us and give us every opportunity to improve and develop our skills and capabilities. Most of us were still teenagers, and he knew how to instruct us and prepare us for war.

Enter the Infantry: 4 RAR in Borneo operated four tracker dogs, Gunnar, Rank, Simba and Toddy. These dogs tracked and also acted as a reconnaissance platoon when required. In dense jungle the dogs could pick up the trail from the visual trackers and go like hell in pursuing the scent, often at times dragging the handlers around, through or over the massive buttress roots of gigantic trees.

What was a little disconcerting was that on many occasions the trackers and the dogs were not believed because many pursuits resulted in nil enemy forces located. Unfortunately, this lack of knowledge and appreciation of the dogs' abilities caused misunderstanding of their true abilities. In hindsight we know now the Indonesians were aware that the dogs were after them and therefore escaped back over to their side of the border and in the main were kept there, where we wanted them. In South Vietnam, 4 RAR would work with tracker dogs again, acting in the tracker reconnaissance roles, with Milo, Trajan and Marcus on the first tour and Milo and Marcian on the regiment's second tour.

Operations also had their lighter moments. While operating in Borneo in the region between Stass and the Gunong Raya, a platoon patrolling the border where the Sungai Separan crosses into Indonesia found a recently vacated rest position. It looked as if the Indonesians had changed dressings on a casualty and then moved on. A tracker team, commanded by Sergeant Jimmy Wild, was immediately flown in to join the platoon. All seven members of the team, plus a Labrador tracker dog, were lifted in one Scout helicopter (showing the versatility of that small helicopter). The dog and dog handler were seated in the bubble of the helicopter, where the co-pilot's seat had been removed, and the other six were crammed into the small cabin. Marshalling the helicopter at the Landing Zone, the platoon commander was alarmed by the erratic approach of the chopper, flown by Australian Army pilot Lieutenant Bob Hills of 7 Reconnaissance Flight. Coming to an unstable hover just in front of him, the chopper made an undignified and less than graceful landing, dropping the last few feet with a thud. The cause of the erratic flight was soon revealed. The dog had scrambled onto the pilot's lap during the flight and in the confined cockpit, the dog handler could not retrieve the dog. With its front paws on the pilot's shoulders, this large dog was showing his delight at the flight by attempting to lick Hill's face as he manoeuvred the aircraft into the Landing Zone.

VIETNAM

During the Vietnam War, the Australian Army provided two units of tracker dogs that were trained by the Tracking Wing of the School of Infantry. When Australia's involvement in Vietnam ended the unit was disbanded.

The dog tracker teams in Vietnam were hated by the Viet Cong (VC) and regarded as a valuable target. A bounty was placed on the heads of both dog and handler. The dogs lived and worked with their handlers, sharing every danger, unaware that men's lives often depended on their ability to do their job. It was inevitable that a very close and strong bond developed. Unlike their human counterparts, the length of duty for a tracker dog was around three years. As infantry battalions rotated every 12 months, the dogs were simply passed on to relieving units. An example of a dog's tour of duty is 'Trajan', donated to the Army by a grandmother from Lawson in the Blue Mountains. He was initially trained by Private Russell McDonald as a tracker dog. He was deployed to South Vietnam with 4 RAR/NZ in 1968 with Private Dennis Symington. Later he served with 6 RAR/NZ being reunited with his original trainer Russell McDonald, followed by 2 RAR/NZ 1970–1971 and finally with 3 RAR in 1971. Trajan's fate is still unknown. Due to government policy at the time, the dogs were not permitted to return to Australia, despite offers by individual handlers to pay all associated quarantine costs and a public campaign to bring all the dogs home (sufficient funds had been raised to do so). After much discussion of the issue and the matter having been raised in Parliament, it was officially decided that at the end of their working lives the dogs would be kept by the battalion as a reserve, then given as pets to European or Australian families resident in Saigon. Records indicate that every effort was made by the Australian Army to ensure the dogs went to good homes. To this day, the fate of Australia's war dogs that served during the Vietnam conflict remains an emotive issue.

The dogs were the core of combat tracker teams that were used from 1967 until the last combat troops left in late 1971. Trained from the age of about 10 months at the Tracking Wing of the Ingleburn Infantry Centre, NSW, two dogs were assigned to each of the Australian battalions based at the Task Force base at Nui Dat, in Phuoc Tuy province. Full-time use of the dogs in Vietnam from late 1967 followed their successful use in Malaya in the 1950s and a trial in Vietnam during most of 1967. Housed in kennels at Nui Dat, the dogs' lives followed an established routine. They were groomed and checked every day, and taken outside the base perimeter for training runs on tracks set through the bush. South Vietnamese soldiers were usually used to set scent trails, so the dogs could get used to following their distinctive smell.

Eleven tracker dogs were deployed to South Vietnam during the Vietnam War: Caesar, Cassius, Janus, Julian, Juno, Justin, Marcian, Marcus, Milo, Tiber and Trajan. They were the six black Labradors and five cross-breed tracker dogs. Cassius was the only Australian tracker dog to die on active service in Vietnam.

Originally a guide dog named Cobber who was too boisterous, he was renamed Cassius and was the first trail tracker dog deployed to South Vietnam in 1967. He had a highly successful career locating Vietcong fighters and enemy installations with 7 RAR.

Each tracker team, consisting of the two dogs and their handlers, two visual trackers and two cover men (a machine-gunner and a signaller), operated on standby out of Nui Dat. Usually called out to follow up enemy trails or to locate suspected enemy hideouts after a contact, the teams would be airlifted by helicopter into the area of operation. The dogs loved these helicopter flights, finding the cool air a relief from the oppressive tropical heat. Once on the ground, the tracker dog would be put on to the scent of the retreating enemy. This meant that the tracker team would lead actual fighting elements towards the enemy – one of the most dangerous jobs in any war, requiring both excellent scouting skills as well as absolute confidence in the tracker dog's ability to sense the enemy before actual contact was made.

The dog would follow the scent until a location was found, at which time he would indicate with a nose or paw extended in a 'point' facing the suspected enemy. Each of the tracker dogs had different ways of pointing: often the 'point' was only a very subtle change in the dog's demeanor, which the tracker team relied upon the dog's handler to interpret. Consequently, the bond between handler and dog in these instances was crucial. The handler and his dog would then fall back while the rest of the section searched the area, often finding wounded enemy or recently occupied bunker systems that would otherwise have been missed.

The dogs were outstandingly successful at their combat tasks in Vietnam. Apart from their success in locating the enemy and their support systems, the dogs saved the lives of their handlers and team members on many occasions. Although not trained to detect mines (despite recommendations by some soldiers that mine dogs be used in Vietnam), the dogs were intelligent and sufficiently well-trained to do so. Some dogs could, according to their handlers, detect the wind breeze over a trip wire and indicate its presence. There are many stories from Vietnam telling of dogs actually standing on their handlers' feet so that they would not take that extra pace that would mean tripping a mine or walking into an enemy ambush; of dogs detecting trip wires, and of working so hard to please that they were physically exhausted and had to be carried by their handlers. Our dogs not only worked with us but worked with many American units and were feted and acclaimed for their ability by all.

The handlers had to carry the extra food and water for their dogs and it was not uncommon to see the dogs drink from the same canteens as their handlers or eat from the same spoons and 'Dixies' (combination plate, mug and pan). The riflemen often shared their rations and water with the handler and the dog but never accepted the offer of food from the handler. The dogs developed empathy not only with their handlers but with all members of the battalion. Many times a very wet and tired handler and dog would sleep together at night with the dog placed upwind by the handler to protect against the cold wind, only for the handler to wake up in the morning shivering with cold and the dog sleeping downwind snuggled up warmly; on other occasions, the handler would dig a separate pit for the dog only to wake up sharing his own pit with the dog.

One officer serving in Vietnam with dogs was Leo Van De Kamp, who joined the Australian Regular Army (ARA) in 1961. On graduation he was posted to 1 RAR as a rifleman. In June 1966, Leo was commissioned at the rank of second lieutenant and was posted to 2 RAR at Enoggera in Queensland. On arrival,

Leo was allocated as the platoon commander of the Anti-Tank Platoon (ATK PL) in Support Company (Spt Coy). However, because there was very little call for anti-tank warfare in Vietnam, the ATK PL was dual-purposed as the Tracking Platoon. In 1965 Leo undertook the tracking team commanders' course. It was a two-week course based on the experiences taken from the Malayan Emergency and had a strong British Army influence in its content and delivery. This was followed by a visual tracking course. About half of Leo's platoon were trained in visual tracking (VT) and acting as 'coverman' to protect the VT and dog handlers. Leo took his whole tracker team, which included two dog teams, to the Infantry Centre and completed a tracker team course in readiness for deployment to South Vietnam. The two dog teams comprising Private Peter Haran and his dog Caesar, and Private Denis Ferguson and his dog Marcus. At that time they were still part of the Tracking Wing, but were fully integrated into the platoon during this course.

At the end of the tracker team course, Leo's team was deployed by RAAF C130 aircraft to Vietnam with the 2 RAR advance party. The remainder of Leo's platoon left Brisbane on board the HMAS *Sydney* on 30 May 1967. Ten days later the battalion arrived at Vung Tau and was moved to the 1st Australian Task Force (1 ATF) base at Nui Dat by CH-47 Chinook helicopters. 2 RAR relieved 6 RAR. The ATK/Tracker PL was ready to go to war. However, there was one glaring omission from the peacetime training of the trackers. They had never trained the trackers with the rifle companies on exercises in Australia. It was to be a steep learning curve for all concerned. In Leo's words: 'I had the unenviable job of convincing the company commanders to use the trackers in the field.' It took a 2 RAR tracker team supporting American forces to convince the Australian commanders that the trackers and their dogs were a valuable asset. The tracker team, including Peter Haran and Caesar, supported the US Army 11th Airborne Cavalry Regiment (11 ACR) and were very successful in following up the enemy after a contact. They travelled for several kilometres through a variety of jungle conditions and then Caesar indicated the presence of enemy soldiers to their immediate front. The Americans attacked and it was a successful operation. News of this success swept through the Australian units like wildfire. The trackers' life now turned full cycle and they were called out on numerous occasions for tracking duties in support of 2 RAR operations. The excitement was in the bush. But Leo, as the platoon commander, found himself coordinating the tracking support from a command post in Nui Dat. This was not what he wanted; he preferred to be in the bush with the diggers. So,he requested a transfer from trackers to a rifle platoon so that he could lead diggers at the forward edge of the battle. In October 1967, Leo was transferred to D Coy as a rifle platoon commander.

This did not end his contact with the trackers. In November 1967 Leo's platoon had a major contact with the enemy in the 'Long Green' area of Phouc Tuy Province (the 1 ATF area of operations), and Leo called in a tracker team to follow up an enemy group who were trying to escape away from the site of the contact. The dog followed the enemy trail but Leo was unable to engage the enemy because they had crossed the Song Rai River, which was outside the range of Artillery from the Horseshoe feature and, accordingly, he was not given clearance to follow on. Leo was frustrated by the attitude shown by some commanders about the value of tracking teams in the Vietnam War. He believes that the success of tracker teams could have been more pronounced had there been a better understanding of their employment.

In January 1968, Leo RTA took on a posting as OC, Tracker Wing at the Infantry Centre at Ingleburn. He set about making some changes to the training content so that it included a greater emphasis on the Vietnam requirement compared with the Malayan Emergency style of training. Leo remained at the Tracker Wing for two years during which time, in July 1969, he was promoted to lieutenant. The kennel area was improved during Leo's time there and he also acquired much experience in tracker dog training techniques.

Life was busy in the Tracking Wing. There was an ongoing process of selecting volunteer dog handlers from the graduating Corps training courses as well as the acquisition of suitable dogs to undertake tracking training. The training of dogs and their handlers was a long and difficult task with a significant number of both dogs and handlers failing to meet the mark. There were numerous courses for tracker platoon commanders, visual trackers, tracker dogs, and tracker teams. Leo had oversight for the training of the RAR battalions' tracking capabilities, and he saw quite a number of these personnel pass through the Wing on their way to the war in South Vietnam.

How our dogs affected the outcome of the engagements in which Australian troops were involved will never be fully understood or recorded. They did cause some enemy to pay the supreme sacrifice for their country, they did prevent our soldiers from becoming casualties and we know that they caused the enemy to change their attitude and intentions from time to time. What we will never be able to prove is how many of our soldiers' lives they saved, how many times they prevented us from being surprised if not annihilated and how many times they were responsible for our successes.

Our country's initial trend to borrow MWDs from others has been completely reversed. The use of Explosive Detection Dogs (EDD) in current operations throughout the world has proved a vital force protection enhancer and Australian forces as well as British, US and other coalition forces all employ them. During the current Afghanistan War several countries have found they lack this vital component, one being Canada. The ADF have supplemented this shortfall by attaching EDD handlers to Canadian formations. Such is the need for EDD teams that several companies from Sweden and the USA employ civilian EDD handlers (many of them ex-ADF dog handlers) under contract to work alongside military and other agencies to fill this shortfall.

2.

DOGS SERVING THE ADF

Of the 4000 or so mammals on the planet, the dog has always been close to us. There are 1.2 million dogs born every day, with a population of over 400 million throughout the world. Only about ten breeds have found a place within our armed forces. The most common are the German and Belgian Shepherds, the Labrador and the Aussie mutt. The troops in Afghanistan even adopted local dogs as mascots for their battalions (although this is officially frowned upon).

There is no perfect war dog, of course, and many a mongrel has served the colours with heroic distinction. In particular, the Army Engineers have had great success with Kelpie crosses, Labrador crosses and Springer Spaniels. Recently, several cross-breed dogs that had been given a second chance from a dog pound have served with distinction in Afghanistan searching for explosives. Many have given the ultimate sacrifice. One such dog was Herbie, who was recruited from the Redcliffe District Dog Pound and is described as a Border Collie cross Husky. He had the structure of the Border Collie and the beautifully soft coat of a Husky. He had an enormous work ethic and searched thoroughly and quickly. In the week before he was killed in action, he and his handler Darren Smith located a large IED along a road. It is understood that they also located some caches containing ammunition. Herbie was farewelled from Tarin Kowt Military Camp with full military honours. He was cremated and his ashes were returned to Australia under Australian quarantine and customs regulations.

These Aussie cross-breed dogs have a long history as working dogs. There were very few cattle in the colony of Australia before the early the 1820s, and thus little need for working dogs because stock was kept in timbered enclosures near the settler's homes. The early dogs in Australia mostly originated from near the ports of southern England, from where ships sailed to the colony. By the 1830s, when the country was opened up by early 'squatters' (pastoral property owners) and drovers, they realised the need to improve on the dogs they had. Thomas Hall, stud master for the Hall family's pastoral holdings, which was the first large cattle empire in the colony, imported his dogs from England. They were called Northumberland Drover's dogs. These dogs bite severely and always attack at the heels of cattle, so that fierce bull were easily driven by them. They are singularly quick and prompt in their actions and they are both courageous and intelligent. These Northumberland Drover's dogs were crossed with Australia's own fully acclimatised and genetically evolved dog, the Dingo, reputed for his silent approach and endurance to heat. This cross resulted in a successful type of dog known as Hall's Heelers (also known at that time as Merlins) or Blue Heelers.

Pure-bred Dingos may not be used in Australia as a MWD but, like many of the worlds' native dogs, they have been used as a cross breed to try and develop the ideal military dog. EDD

Axle was the last of the active response dogs to be retained by RAE. An active response dog is allowed to become excited over the discovery of a stimulus – not a good idea when working with tripwires or touchy pressure-plate fired bombs. Axle was a German Shepherd cross Dingo. Dr Rudolphina Menzel, a noted authority on dogs, emigrated to Palestine (the future state of Israel) in 1934. She was asked by the Haganah, Israel's first defence force, to develop a service dog organisation for guarding the isolated Hebrew settlements and fighting the war of independence. Finding that the breeds traditionally used for war tasks suffered impaired efficiency from the adverse climatic conditions, Dr Menzel turned her attention to the pariah dogs (semi-wild or feral dogs) she found living in the area. She concluded that this was a true native breed of dog ideally adapted to the conditions of this difficult land. She named the breed the 'Canaan', after the Land of Canaan.

Dr Menzel first began working with wild and semi-wild adult dogs near her home by luring them with food. She also captured litters of puppies, which she raised and found extraordinarily adaptable to domestication. She then began her own breeding program and introduced the Canaan as a MWD. The Canaan was used extensively during and after World War II for patrol, tracking and guard work. One of the first dogs trained to detect mines effectively was a Canaan dog. After the war Dr Menzel successfully trained several Canaans as seeing-eye dogs. Today some follow that tradition by serving as therapy dogs. As in times past, the Canaan can today be found guarding Bedouin camps and flocks. The Israeli public has also come to appreciate the qualities of its native breed and so these dogs are in great demand as home guard dogs. The Israel Defense Force continues to rely on the Canaan for guard and patrol work. Although pure

Canaans still exist in a wild and semi-wild state, their numbers are dwindling due to the encroachment of civilisation. This dog looks remarkably similar to the Australian Dingo.

The German Shepherd (also known as an Alsatian), is a large-sized breed that originated in Germany. The German Shepherd is a relatively new breed and its origins date to 1899. As part of the herding group of dogs, the German Shepherd developed originally for herding sheep. Because of their strength, intelligence and abilities in obedience training, they are often employed in police and military roles in forces around the world. The German Shepherd is a very popular selection for use as a working dog. It is especially well known for its police work, being used for tracking criminals, patrolling troubled areas, and detection and holding of suspects. Additionally, thousands of German Shepherds have been used by the military, including in Australia. Usually trained for scout duty, the dog is used to warn soldiers of the presence of enemies or booby traps or other hazards. The German Shepherd is one of the most commonly used breeds in a wide variety of scent-work roles, including search and rescue, cadaver searching, and the detection of narcotics, explosives, accelerants and mines. The dog is suited for these lines of work because of its keen sense of smell and ability to work, regardless of distractions. Three German Shepherds served in Somalia with the Engineers.

The modern Labrador's ancestors originated on the island of Newfoundland, now part of the province of Newfoundland and Labrador, Canada. The breed emerged over time from the St John's water dog, also an ancestor of the Newfoundland dog (to which the Labrador is closely related). Labradors are an intelligent breed with a good work ethic and generally good temperaments. They also have a great sense of smell. Common working roles for

Labradors include hunting, tracking and detection, guide dogs, police and military working dogs.

During Vietnam most of our dogs were black, which was an ideal camouflage in the jungle. Their social temperament of not being a one-man dog allowed them to freely mix with the other soldiers of the battalion and their cross breeding improved their endurance. Probably the most famous of all Australian tracker dogs worldwide was Caesar, who was a Labrador Kelpie cross.

The Belgian Shepherd (Malinois) is sometimes classified as a variety of the Belgian Shepherd dog rather than as a separate breed. In Belgium, Germany, the Netherlands and other European countries, as well as in the USA, Canada and Australia, the Malinois is bred primarily as a working dog for personal protection, drug and explosive detection, police work and search and rescue. The RAAF use the largest numbers of this breed within the ADF as they seem well-suited to hot climates and are full of energy.

Several countries have deliberately bred MWD in a mottled colour to assist in camouflage and concealment. Gone are the days of WWI when white dogs were painted black so not to stand out. In the 1970s the ADF even conducted research in Australia into the genetic possibility of breeding the perfect MWD: one that has all the scenting, fitness, silence, aggression and colour traits needed in a war dog.

The majority of Kelpie-like dogs are generally described as Kelpies whether they were directly traceable to the foundation or not. There is little question that the Kelpie is an Australian version of the short and/or smooth-coated working Collie, the foundation being mainly black-and-tan or black dogs carrying very little white. The modern, top-quality working Kelpie is traceable to the early foundation stock in the 1870s. It is a short-coated, prick-eared dog who revels in hard going. Established especially for local conditions, it is able to muster huge areas under extreme conditions, often doing without water for hours on end. Derived from a long line of working dogs and capable of handling thousands of sheep at a time, the Kelpie has a highly developed ability to solve problems for itself, and actually prefers to do so. The Kelpie appears to have been immediately suited to the harsh Australian conditions.

It is not surprising then that the Army Engineers tasked with searching in Afghanistan look very favourably on the Kelpie and use them along with Kelpie cross-breeds in those harsh conditions.

3.

MILITARY CANINE BREEDING

The RAAF spent the first 40 years using dogs relying on the public to hand over unwanted pets. These donations, according to head of the K-9 Development Team, Flight Sergeant Alan Grossman, led to major problems with quality control: 'The dogs we'd usually get were around two years old, and some were quite aggressive.'

Procurement of suitable canines for MWD development and training was becoming a critical issue at the Military Working Dog Training Flight at RAAF Base Amberley. The traditional recruiting base was diminishing and existing breeders and vendors could not meet demands, particularly given the popularity of this type of canine with other agencies.

In 2001 the RAAF proposed to set up a pilot program to assess the viability of breeding suitable canines for training as MWDs. The program was supported and endorsed and the Canine Breeding Cell began operation in 2003. The Canine Breeding Cell at RAAF Base Amberley now produces the majority of dogs required to meet course needs within the RAAF. Due to the numbers bred and to aid administration in identifying dogs in the future, puppies are given names starting with their litter letter, for example D for Delta. The puppies will be under the care of the team in the breeding cell until they are three months old, and then will join the foster care program. MWD puppies are then raised by families to ensure they grow up in normal circumstances with exposure to the sights and sounds of the world. This gives the dogs a rounded life and helps selection at the final stage prior to entering service. Even so, not all puppies bred will pass the final selection stage to spend the rest of their lives guarding the valuable assets of the RAAF. However, this method is still more cost-efficient than relying on donated dogs (because perhaps only one in 30 may be suitable). In 2010 the RAAF opened a new state-of-the-art MWD facility incorporating breeding, isolation, veterinary and kennel areas worth $5 million. The main breeds in the RAAF breeding program are German and Belgian Shepherds. The RAAF also supplies dogs to other services, including the Queensland Police Service.

Flight Sergeant Grossman explained that one of the biggest challenges of the breeding program is not finding willing participants but working through the adoptive families' concerns about becoming too attached to their new friends: 'I'd be worried if there wasn't a tear or two when we went to collect the puppy – it means they've formed a bond, and a strong bond makes for a great learning environment.'

It is hoped in the future that semen from MWDs from around the world can be stored in an international sperm bank and used to continually improve the breeding programs of the military.

In the early 1970s the SME dog breeding program was assisted by the Department of Animal Husbandry of the CSIRO, with Dr Barrie Latter acting as the consulting geneticist. Dr Latter provided SME with the technical processes for adopting a combination of line-breeding, outcrossing and inbreeding which could, after ten dog generations (20 years), produce a genotypic special military breed of dog with a number of military characteristics. These included: small size, light weight, agility, courage, high olfactory capabilities, strong retrieval instinct and the ability to work off-leash and by electronic remote-control. The colour requested for the dogs, was deep olive-bronze-green. The colour was an item that Dr Latter doubted could be achieved, but accepted a modified choice of at least a dark coat with possibly a disruptive pattern in it, such as a sable or black-and-tan.

The initial breed stock was acquired using Dr Latter's breed criteria and the first pups were born in June 1972 at the SME kennels under the watchful eye of Sergeant Ray Wilson. The pups were introduced to handling, noises, explosive aromas and other military stimuli from a few days after birth. The records indicated that the time when the pups began demonstrating their best responses to military stimuli was when they reached 21 days of age. In addition, the pups in the litter were encouraged to follow their mother, a fully trained EDD, when she was searching for explosives and trip wires during a training run. The pups saw their mother being rewarded for detecting explosives and trip wires and began exhibiting behaviour which indicated that they wanted to be a 'part of the action' too. Employing this 'operant conditioning' procedure, the pups learned very quickly what was required of them. The combination breeding-and-training system was planned so that the progeny would provide very high quality detection canines in the shortest possible time. The breeding program continued on for another three generations until 1980, but due to pressures on the RAE, it was abandoned. The results were never measured and the outcomes of the research were left without a final evaluation.

The Army Military Police (MP) look for all-round working dogs, and have no role for specialist detection dogs at this time. Dogs must be bold enough to engage a combatant when required and to protect their handlers; however, overly aggressive dogs are useless – in fact, they are a liability because teams must work closely with other soldiers on patrols. Gone are the days of 'land sharks'.

The Army MWDs are obtained via donation or sourced from animal rescue shelters. Some ads are posted in veterinary clinics and magazines. The selection process is as difficult as handler selection because only the best dogs will be accepted. Testing is done in an unfamiliar environment to assess a dog's self-confidence. Tests include chasing instinct (retrieving a thrown object), tug-of-war games and noise sensitivities (essential in dogs used on a battlefield).

The Army Engineers purchases or accepts donations of 'green' dogs – that is, dogs with no prior detection training. Dogs must be 18 months old, physically fit, healthy and bold but not aggressive. Most dogs tend to fail assessment or the training program due to a lack of 'prey drive' or a continued lack of intense desire for the reward, such as a tennis ball. The intensity sought in a candidate is extremely important as EDDs are often expected to work in arduous, oppressive, humid tropical conditions, without rest for up to 40 minutes at a time with little or no reward. They are then expected to recover quickly and go back to work until the task is complete. Without natural drive, intensity and determination, most dogs will give up under such conditions. Other dogs fail for variety of reasons, including inferior scenting ability or bad reactions to stressful environments that cannot be counter-conditioned. All training is conducted at the SME at Moorebank, Sydney. Training takes 19 weeks before the new dog is teamed with its first handler. The first handler will usually conduct continuation training with that dog for a further six months before the team is ready to sit the Operational Assessment. Once the team passes this assessment, it is ready for live operation at home or abroad in a high-threat environment.

The role of the breeds within the ADF also varies. There are two main types of MWD in Australia. Basically they are broken down into specialist search dogs – in this case Explosive Detection Dogs (EDD). Used by the Army Engineers and RAAF, these MWDs can detect minuscule amounts of a wide range of explosives, making them an invaluable addition both to entry points and patrolling within secure installations. These dogs are capable of achieving a very high success rate in bomb detection. They are also in demand patrolling ahead of troops on the roadside where suspect IED may be present.

The predominant MWDs, at least as far as numbers are concerned, are used by the RAAF and Army Military Police and perform a variety of functions, from patrolling, tracking, search, obedience, agility and attack work. Over the history of war dog use, Australia has used dogs in many roles as messengers, mine detection, haulage dogs and, up until recent times, narcotic detection.

Australian soldiers always look after their dogs as a matter of priority, no matter what their breed. After a long day patrolling, the Aussie dog is looked after before his master takes a break. Australian servicemen have always had a rapport with animals on the battlefield. Whether as a mascot or official MWD or the local stray pet, diggers have found comfort in animal companionship during war. Like their human counterparts, MWDs need rest away from foot or vehicle traffic between patrols. It can therefore be a lonely job for them as far as human contact is concerned, often working on point or alone searching for explosive devices.

MWD accommodation ranges from a simple ventilated portable kennel as used by EDD teams from 2 CER in Afghanistan, to their own tent, and even more elaborate semi-permanent kennels like those used in East Timor. In the true Australian tradition, most of the supplies to make these kennels were 'liberated' from people who really didn't need the materials in the first place. Diggers did their own carpentry and concreting with homemade plumbing and drainage to boot.

Dog Handlers

There are two elements to an effective military working dog team: one human and one canine. The careful selection of people suitable for training as dog handlers is vital to the successful employment of dogs for military purposes. There are some differences between services. In the RAAF Police and Military Police, as their name would indicate, members must be service police personnel first. In both these units a MWD handler is one of several job descriptions within the service police mustering. Handlers must complete various service police courses and even a specified time period before seeking selection as a dog handler. However, in the Australian Army Engineers, dog handlers are volunteers who have completing basic combat engineer training and are members of that corps. In the RAAF you can spend your entire career from airman to warrant officer in the MWD trade. Similarly, in the MPs and Engineers you can remain a 'doggie' all your service; however, due to their limited numbers promotion can be slow and to attain higher rank you may have to leave the dog mustering.

In Australia there has never been a shortage of servicemen who came from the country. During the colonial and empire wars, recruiters would traditionally seek out stockmen and farmers for the mounted units. These same men were regarded as having the skills necessary to work with dogs. During WWI, when Australian units first decided to explore the use of war dogs, these same practical hands-on men used to working with animals were first sought out. When recruiting MWD handlers, I looked for the same practical, independent can-do attribute generally found in people raised in the country. In those raised in the city, these abilities are usually known as 'street smarts'. Previous experience with animals may well be an advantage but the lack of it is not necessarily a disqualification in the case of an otherwise suitable candidate.

Most 'doggies' tend to be of a junior non-commissioned officer (JNCO) rank by virtue of their job, but they are regularly required to brief much higher ranking officers as the subject-matter expert and advise them on canine matters, including tactics. To do such things dog handlers must gain the respect of their superiors, a job made easier if they are self-reliant, professional and highly motivated.

ADF personnel considered as suitable MWD handlers must have sound military core skills, preferably from an Infantry background, and possess mental alertness, have an equable temperament and the ability to work unsupervised under isolated and extreme circumstances. The nature of the training and subsequent operational work calls for a high standard of physical fitness. It is no good having all the academic qualifications in the world if you cannot lift a dog over a 2-metre fence or carry your injured partner of 40 kilograms to a medical facility several kilometres away. Fitness is a major consideration for both dog and handler during tactical operations. Many missions require operating away from the Base of Operations (BOP) for days at a time. During this time a handler must not only carry all his personnel equipment, including rations, water and weapons, but also all of his canine's needs, such as food, additional water, harness, leads, bowls, booties, goggles, K9 first aid and any other item required for the mission.

Of course MWD handling is not the total domain of men. A Military Police female dog handler, Corporal Carmen Thompson, was attached to 4 RAR assigned to Balibo, on the border with West Timor in 2001 and was the first female in the ADF to handle a MWD on active service. The Military Police graduated two female MWD handlers in 2011 and the Combat Engineers have a female EDD handler for the first time on course the same year.

The RAAF have had female MWD handlers for many years. Corporal Vanessa Wallis is the first woman in the history of the Australian Defence Force to handle a MWD with a bullet in the chamber of her rifle and ready to take her part in a firefight, during a combat situation. Vanessa comes from the Ipswich area of Queensland and spent most of her formative years mixing city and country living together. She has had a love of animals, particularly dogs, from a very early age. When she was seven, her school took her to see the RAAF police dog demonstration at the RAAF Base at Amberley. At the end of the demonstration Vanessa made up her mind that she wanted to become a MWD handler in the RAAF. In 2002, after initial recruit training, she was posted to RAAF Base Amberley where she graduated from the RAAF Security and Fire School as a MWD handler.

On graduation, Vanessa was teamed up with her first dog, PD Kirra. A short time later Kirra passed away from a veterinary problem. Vanessa was then teamed up with her second MWD, German Shepherd Akyra, and they have been a team ever since. Her first posting as a RAAF security person was with 382 Expeditionary Combat Support Squadron (ECSS) base at RAAF Amberley where she and Akyra patrolled the base and conducted sensitive area security duties.

Overseas Service

In early 2006 the threat to peace and stability in East Timor had become an international issue. At that time 382 ECSS was the standby unit to deploy and when the call came to deploy to East Timor, 382 ECSS mobilised. The mobilisation included six MWD teams, in which Leading Aircraftwoman Vanessa Wallis was one of the personnel to go, with her dog Akyra. Vanessa's group were airlifted to Darwin by C130 (Hercules) transport aircraft in May 2006 where they commenced training and acclimatisation for their on-movement to East Timor. This training included long-distance marches with full combat loads in the heat of the day in the Darwin area. When the order came for the dog unit to deploy to East Timor, Sergeant Shane 'Kiwi' Campbell and Corporal Brett Thompson were sent to East Timor with their dogs to arrange for the reception of the remainder of the dog unit, which followed 48 hours later. There were a few issues to address initially with the administrative and logistic support for overseas dog deployments such as this one for East Timor. The time came for the movement of the remaining four RAAF dog handlers and their dogs. The handlers were Corporal Brett, Corporal Allen, Leading Aircraftman Luckman and Leading Aircraftwoman Wallis. The group was loaded onto a RAAF C130 (Hercules) aircraft and arrived at Komoro airport near Dili just on midnight. As there were intelligence reports that there may have been a chance of hostile fire being directed at the aircraft, a tactical landing was executed. In Vanessa's words:

The four of us were at the back door of the aircraft and the dogs were in containers in front of us. We were fully kitted up for action with weapons, live rounds, Kevlar body protection and field packs. The loadmaster came to us at the rear of the aircraft and told us to prepare for action and that we were about to land. His instructions included 'put on your helmets'. That was very difficult because the helmets were attached to the packs on our backs. So we sat and looked at each other and wondered what the heck we had let ourselves in for. Immediately the aircraft touched down we were ordered to 'load', and onto our rifles went a full magazine.

The aircraft had barely stopped when the cargo hatch was lowered and we told to get off quickly. After sitting in the cold of the Hercules from Darwin, the heat and the smell of East Timor hit us as a sudden surprise, given that most of us had never been outside Australia before. The Hercules kept its motors revving and the crew were obviously getting ready to load up again and then take off. Our gear and dogs were removed from the aircraft very swiftly by the airlift team.

I had a problem moving because we had been sitting for a long time without the opportunity to move about, then the weight of the pack and the need to move quickly on numb legs and jump the 20 centimetres from the ramp onto the tarmac was a far bigger effort than I had imagined it would be. I was helped down from the ramp by some kind soul who could see my predicament. The dogs were still in their containers and the containers were lashed to a pallet. The pallet was removed by a forklift and we saw our dogs disappear into the darkness. Sergeant Campbell and Corporal Thompson were there to receive us and helped us to keep together and reunite us with our dogs.

The RAAF MWD section spent a few days in that area before being allocated a building in the airport precinct. Their initial job was to guard the evacuation centre so that foreign civilians, including Australians, could be air-transported out of the country without the aircraft being rushed by desperate East Timorese people. Other tasks included the removal of local people from areas needed by the security forces. The local people knew that the international troops were not about to open fire on them, so they were very slow to respond to demands to move on. However, when the dog section turned up they moved very quickly. Apparently, they were afraid of large dogs, such as the German Shepherd. This was handy when the large carparks adjacent to the airport were being cleared of people and illicit weapons. Suspicious people and armed civilians were quickly rounded up and handed over to the security forces. There is no doubt that the dogs were a boon in this function. There was a lot of gang violence, spontaneous riots and rock throwing going on at the time. Many of these incidents were pacified the moment the dogs arrived as the dog section was instrumental in assisting the security forces to separate out the opposing factions.

Some RAAF MWD patrols assisted the Australian Federal Police while they patrolled the general area and eventually they saw some Army MP dogs in the area also. However, they were unable to join forces with the MP because their tasks were located in the city of Dili guarding the gaols and other sensitive areas. The RAAF had been allocated security duties in the airport area.

The dogs had to be administered in line with Australian Quarantine Inspection Service (AQIS) protocols, which included daily and bi-weekly medications, and dipping every three days. This was to combat the possibility of pathogenic parasites being present in the dogs. Every dose, type of medication and dipping regime had to be annotated and certified in writing for monitoring by AQIS personnel. LACW Wallis was assigned the responsibility of packaging the medications for her compatriot handlers as well as reminding them of the timing for dips. Her previous experience in civilian dog kennels came in handy in East Timor. The dog food was packaged in 20 kilogram bags and came from Australia. However, dry dog food is a magnet for rats and mice and it was a constant battle to protect the dog food from the abundant vermin in the area.

Village Incident

Leading Aircraftwoman Vanessa Wallis went on a patrol with three Airfield Defence Group airmen (ADGs).

Their task was to patrol the area near a village close to the airport. On arrival, the patrol saw a commotion going on with the local people and an armed suspect. The suspect saw the patrol and ran off. The ADG commander gave the order to pursue him and so the three ADGs, Vanessa and Vanessa's dog, Akyra, gave immediate chase, straight into the village. The ADGs began to close on the suspect because he had to run between civilians who, seeing the problem, began screaming and running for cover. However, the ADG commander realised that the suspect might be running his patrol into an ambush. So the commander ordered his patrol to go to 'action' with their weapons. Vanessa cocked her weapon and for the first time in her life realised that she might have to fight her way out of a dangerous situation. They continued the chase with adrenalin pumping, her finger on the safety catch and Akyra ready to go into action if Vanessa so much as burped. At one point the patrol almost tackled the suspect, but he turned a corner and ran straight into the arms of another group of soldiers from the international security forces and was captured. It was not his day. But the RAAF patrol breathed a collective sigh of relief as they 'made safe' their rifles.

Reinforcements from the MWD section at RAAF Base Richmond began to arrive about three weeks after the RAAF Base Amberley MWD team arrived in the country. There were four reinforcement airmen with their dogs from Richmond who travelled to East Timor aboard the HMAS *Kanimbla*.

After several months deployment the dogs had to be made ready for their return to Australia under the strict AQIS protocols and veterinary arrangements for that move. Two of the handlers were assigned to escort the eight dogs back through the AQIS process of certification and quarantine en route to, and on arrival in Australia. The remaining six, including Vanessa, were tasked to pack up, clean their equipment and area and prepare themselves for their own return home.

In 2008, Vanessa Wallis was posted as an instructor to the RAAF Security and Fire School at Amberley. Her current posting is at RAAF Base Darwin.

4.

DOG TAILS

The following chapter includes several stories about war dogs and their handlers throughout Australia's conflicts. Permission to use these stories has kindly been given by the people involved or the Australian Defence Force Tracker and War Dog Association. I start with the story of Sarbi who came to media attention after surviving in hostile enemy terrain for over a year before returning back to the colours. Sarbi was not the first ADF MWD to suffer this fate – a similar thing happened in Malaya to MWD Tex, who decided to chase the Communist terrorist (CT) into the jungle by himself, only to return many days later.

AFGHANISTAN: EDD SARBI

Sarbi is an Australian Special Forces EDD who spent almost 14 months missing in action (MIA) in Afghanistan, having disappeared during an ambush on 2 September 2008. Sarbi had been wounded in the ambush and had in fact returned to a nearby International Security Assistance Force (ISAF) forward operating base, but was reportedly chased away by Afghan guards.

Sarbi, a black Australian Labrador cross, aged about four, was rescued by an American serviceman who was aware that Australian Special Forces soldiers were missing one of their EDDs. Sarbi was located at an isolated patrol base in north-eastern Oruzgan. The US soldier suspected she was not an enemy combatant, but a highly trained, hairy bomb-sniffing digger and gave Sarbi some commands. When the dog understood, his suspicions were confirmed.

At the time of her disappearance Sarbi was coming to the end of her second tour of duty in Afghanistan, having been deployed to Oruzgan in 2007. Sabi had previously been used by the Incident Response Regiment during the 2006 Commonwealth Games held in Melbourne before being deployed to Afghanistan as part of the Australian Army's Operation Slipper.

Sarbi was present with her handler when their combined Australian, US and Afghan National Army convoy was ambushed by an insurgent force. Nine Australian soldiers, including Sarbi's handler, were wounded SAS Trooper Mark Donaldson won a Victoria Cross in the same battle.

Repeated attempts were made by the Special Operations Task Group to find her. After being located by the US soldier and returned to Australian troops she was flown to Tarin Kowt and reunited with one of her handlers who knew instantly it was Sarbi. 'I nudged a tennis ball to her with my foot and she took it straight away. It's a game we used to play over and over during her training,' the handler said.

Trooper Mark Donaldson said Sarbi's return closed a chapter of their shared history. 'She's the last piece of the puzzle,' he told the Queen, according to British newspaper reports. 'Having Sarbi back gives some closure for the handler and the rest of us who served with her in 2008. It's a fantastic morale booster for the guys.'

Sarbi was taken on board an Aussie C130, which took her from Tarin Kowt to Kandahar where she had a three-day veterinary health check. This was followed by a civilian flight to Dubai in the United Arab Emirates on 1 June, where she spent six months in quarantine.

She was kept in Dubai to prepare her in accordance with Australian Quarantine and Inspection Service import conditions, undergoing vaccinations, testing, treatments and health checks. She came home around Christmas 2010, then went to the AQIS Eastern Creek quarantine facility in NSW for 30 days before returning to her Special Forces unit, the Incident Response Regiment, where she continued her training and assessment for further possible employment as an EDD.

After assessment it was decided she was suffering from post-traumatic stress and has been used by the Explosive Detection Dog School to assist in the training of new dog handler recruits. She will be retired as a much-loved pet with her current handler and his family.

The RSPCA made her the first army dog to be awarded a prestigious Royal Society for the Prevention of Cruelty to Animals' Purple Cross for exceptional service to humans. The black Labrador retriever cross was awarded the Purple Cross in Canberra, in a ceremony attended by Chief of Army, Lieutenant General Ken Gillespie. Sarbi became only the second Australian military animal to receive the country's most prestigious animal bravery award for war-related efforts. The first was the donkey Murphy, also known as 'Simpson's donkey', which was used to ferry the wounded from the WWI battlefield of Gallipoli.

The Purple Cross recognises the deeds of animals that have shown outstanding service to humans, particularly exceptional courage in risking their own safety or life to save a person from injury or death. The award was named to honour the Purple Cross Society, which was established soon after the outbreak of WW II to raise funds for the supply of gear and veterinary treatment for the Light Horse Brigade. The Purple Cross Society was disbanded in 1971 and the RSPCA in Victoria was charged with preserving and displaying the society's flag, which now hangs in the Council Room of the RSPCA Victoria headquarters. As a tribute to the memory of all of Australia's war horses, the RSPCA Australia exceptional animal award is known as the Purple Cross Award. Recipients of the Purple Cross Award receive a Purple Cross medal and a certificate.

Sarbi's RSPCA citation reads:

On the 5 April 2011, Sarbi was awarded an RSPCA Purple Cross Award at the Australian War Memorial. The Australian Special Forces Explosive Detections Dog was declared missing in action September 2008 following a battle with the Taliban which left nine soldiers wounded, including her handler. Sarbi was missing for 13 months, before she was reunited with her handler after being spotted wandering with an Afghan man in north-eastern Oruzgan Province. During her time alone in Afghanistan, Sarbi showed an incredible resilience and strength. And it is her courage and her unquestioning, unwavering service to man that has seen her recognised for a Purple Cross.

A recent check of Sarbi's regimental record revealed that her name has been previously incorrectly spelt in Defence public reporting. The record is now corrected to show the spelling as Sarbi, not 'Sabi'. So popular has Sarbi become she even has her own page on the official government Ministry of Defence website filled with nearly a hundred pictures and messages from fans. It seems everyone from generals to prime ministers and the Governor-General have taken the opportunity to pose with Sarbi.

As wonderful a story as Sarbi's is, five EDDs have been killed in Afghanistan and they deserve medals too – and let us not forget the brave personnel that hold onto their leads. Tragically, at the time of writing another dog has been reported missing. An EDD working with the Special Operations Task Group (SOTG) was missing in action and, regrettably, is likely to be dead after an intense fire fight in northern Helmand province in July 2011. EDD Lucky broke away from a partnered Australian Special Forces and Afghan National Police force heavily engaged with a large number of insurgents.

Lucky went missing during the same battle that took the life of Sergeant Todd Langley.

Commanding officer of the SOTG, Lieutenant Colonel G. (who cannot be named for operational security reasons), said accurate small arms and rocket-propelled grenade fire prevented the immediate safe retrieval of Lucky.

'Unfortunately Lucky was not recovered and, due to the tactical situation on the ground, we were unable to follow up after several hours of intense fighting,' Lieutenant Colonel G. said. The tactical situation was such that it was impossible for the partnered force to safely follow the dog through and beyond the vegetated area insurgents were using as a fighting position.'

Despite repeated attempts to call him back, Lucky was last seen in the vicinity of a major insurgent concentration. The insurgent position was heavily targeted by the SOTG elements using offensive air support during the course of the battle. Post-action analysis of the battle and ongoing monitoring of the region had led Defence to conclude that it was likely that Lucky was killed in the fighting. The team made all reasonable attempts to secure the safe return of Lucky, including repeated calls for the dog on a loudspeaker and broadcasting the offer of a monetary reward in the local area.

'Our dogs are important to our operations and our handlers form extremely close bonds with their dog – losing an EDD is particularly hard on them, but it also affects the whole team who enjoy the company of the dogs,' Lieutenant Colonel G. said.

The Ministry of Defence delayed the release of information concerning Lucky in order to first exhaust all possible efforts to recover the dog and confirm his status after the battle.

SOMALIA

In February 1991, Seamus Doherty arrived at SME to undertake his training as an EDD handler.

At that time, RAE had 30 dogs and 16 dog handlers at SME under the control of 'Smiley' Matthews. There were two dog teams each in the 1st Combat Engineer Regiment (1 CER) at Holsworthy and 3 CER in Townsville. Seamus graduated as an EDD handler, and a short time later, became a dog trainer under the watchful eye of Smiley Matthews. During this period, Seamus was teamed up with EDD Mick. When 3 CER needed a dog team, Seamus volunteered for the job and shortly afterwards he and Mick were posted to 3 CER in Townsville.

In December of 1992, the situation in Somalia had seriously deteriorated, the United States Marine Corps (USMC) had been deployed because non-government organisations (NGOs), such as the United Nations assistance groups, were experiencing difficulties with the collapse of the government. Warlords were traumatising the local population and Somalia was very quickly becoming a 'failed state'. Military help was needed to restore law and order and get aid and administrative services re-established. Australia agreed to send a contingent and mobilised its Operational Deployment Force (ODF) based at Townsville. Seamus and Mick received a week and a half of deployment training and briefings in Townsville before they departed for Somalia in January 1993 by Qantas air charter. The EDD capability included three teams: Seamus Doherty with EDD Mick (German Shepherd), Simon Harvey with EDD Duke (German Shepherd) and Darren Davis with EDD Tia (German Shepherd cross, possibly with Kelpie).

The dogs were transported in portable kennels on the same aircraft as the three handlers. The flight went via Singapore to Mogadishu. They arrived by day and saw a myriad of military aircraft operating around the Mogadishu airport. When the 35 sappers from 3 CER were on the ground, a warrant officer ordered everybody to 'get down' as incoming small arms fire was being received in the airport area. Shots were fired back by the friendly security personnel, and the captain of the Qantas Boeing 747 cargo aircraft got his aircraft out of there as quickly as he possibly could.

That first night, the EDD section was accommodated in a transit camp situated at the end of the runway. A slight mistiming of the ammunition supply meant that the sappers were in position with their personal weapons but had no ammunition. In Seamus's words:

> Throughout the night, there were sounds of firing from small arms, RPGs and very frequent takeoffs and landings from heavy-lift transport aircraft. It was a sleepless night.'

Next morning the ammunition arrived and was quickly distributed. They moved to another part of the airport where we loaded on to United States Air Force C 130 aircraft and flew to the Australian Area of Operations (AO) at Baidoa.

At the Australian camp in Baidoa there didn't appear to be any arrangements for the kennelling of our three dogs. There were five USMC sergeants, who were Explosive Ordnance Disposal (EOD) technicians, with an aircraft as accommodation fully bombed up and fuelled up standing forlornly to one side of the runway. The Marines had tents erected in the aircraft bunds and invited us to move in with them. Our own EOD technician and the ammunition technician moved in as well, so there were five Marines together with five Aussies. The Marines had organised ISO containers for storage and security and had set themselves up very well. We were very grateful to the Americans for their generosity. But the American generosity did not stop there. A few weeks later the Marines had to go back to Mogadishu, and on departure just bequeathed the whole lot to us. The dogs had good shade but we had to keep Mick and Duke away from each other in case they fought. It was very hot during the day where the temperature went into the high 40 degrees Celsius and all the water had to be carried in as bottled water.

Rations for the dogs became an exercise in inventiveness. The EDD team were supposed to have received 25 cartons of dog food – instead they received 25 cans. It was gone in no time and so the dogs were fed on US Army combat rations. Consequently, the dogs lost a lot of condition. Local food arrangements did not work very well either. The Army tried to buy local goats, butcher them and cook up the meat, but that was a lot of work for a small amount of meat. Dog food came on the next logistic ship, and when it did, the diet problem was solved.

The work undertaken by the EDD teams was to support

infantry patrols, mainly in the town of Baidoa. These patrols of up to company strength would spread out through the area and provide extra protection for the international NGO aid agencies in their compounds. In addition, they would activate intelligence reports about the presence of arms and ammunition in the local houses and villages. The infantry would secure the buildings and the EDD teams would search and locate items of interest. Seamus found it easier not to carry a rifle, and preferred his sidearm for personal protection should he ever need to use it. The dogs found a large quantity of arms, ammunition and explosive ordnance in occupied and abandoned buildings and backyard areas. Mick was really good at finding RPG propellant charge packs.

A typical ploy of the insurgents was to mingle with the local people and then fire shots at the security forces. Having done that, they would then dump the weapons in nearby hides (areas where the enemy store or hide weapons) and re-mingle with the locals. The EDD teams would be called out at any time of the day or night immediately after such incidents to search for the abandoned weapons. In open areas and on roads and tracks, the system for searching was the off-leash box pattern process. Building searches were conducted using a set search procedure so that nothing was missed. But for vehicle searches, the dogs were operated as the situation dictated. There were a lot of Italian pattern hand grenades found around the area.

Landmines and IED were not a big issue in the Australian AO, but there were a lot found in hides and caches. The mines were being used mainly on the border of Somalia and Ethiopia, well north of the Australian AO. Sappers did prod for mines when they supported an armoured patrol. When an intelligence report indicated that mines may have been laid, Seamus left Mick behind and worked as a combat engineer. No mines were found.

ABOVE: War Dog 103 Nell, a cross Setter; 102 Trick, a Collie; and 101 Bullet, an Airedale were very efficient in message carrying and saw service with the 2nd, 4th and 5th Australian Divisions in World War I.

ABOVE LEFT: Corporal Bob Madden with Poona, attached to the First Army Experimental Dog Training Unit at Lowanna, NSW, in 1943.

ABOVE RIGHT: The dogs used for training were donated to the Army after publicity in Sydney newspapers. A variety of breeds were used, but the German Shepherd predominated.

BELOW: Private Lance Abbott exercises patrol dog Lux. Originally from Melbourne, Australia, patrol dog Lux served with the British Army in Malaya prior to service in Korea.

ABOVE: Corporal George Gray with patrol dog Eros at the Kansas Line, in Korea, 1953. The Kansas Line was a strategic defensive line approximately 45 kilometres north of Seoul that ran roughly along the 38th parallel.

BELOW: Ray Caulfield and Tutu track, Malaya.

ABOVE: Not much has changed. MWDs patrol ahead of infantry platoons on point, the most dangerous position in the unit. This photo, from Timor-Leste, could be a flashback to Vietnam.

ABOVE: Norm Cameron and Tiba on alert in South Vietnam.

OPPOSITE BELOW: Private Denis 'Fergie' Ferguson with Marcus on the left and Private Peter Haran with Caesar at Nui Dat, South Vietnam, 1967–68.

BELOW LEFT: Jumping from a helicopter into action.

BELOW RIGHT: On point in the Vietnamese jungle.

ABOVE: Private Brett Charlton with Justin (on lead) and RAAF Door Gunner Aircraftsman Rod McKinnon and Tiber, at Fire Support Base Coral, Vietnam, May 1968.

OPPOSITE BELOW: EDD Storm in his winter kit, Afghanistan 2009.

ABOVE LEFT: Due to the lack of vet or a vet corps in the ADF, medics usually go along with the dog handler to treat any canine injuries. ABOVE RIGHT: EDD Kylie is lowered by hand from the HMAS *Diamantina* into the waiting hands of her handler, in August 2003. EDDs are used to conduct searches on vessels which the Navy boards at sea.

LEFT: EDDs were used in Somalia with great effect, even on occasions in crowd control as the local population were scared of dogs. The handler is Seamus Dohnerty.

LEFT: Leading Aircraftman Brendan Dennis of No. 321 Expeditionary Combat Support Squadron (321 ECSS) and EDD Quill conduct a vehicle search.

The local population were Muslim, and Islamic custom is not to allow animals, such as dogs, to come into contact with people or in places where they eat and sleep. Some village heads would complain about this to the Australian commander in an effort to keep the EDDs out of their habitats. The locals called the German Shepherds 'dogs from hell'. They were so determined not to let the dogs into their houses that when the locals realised that the EDDs were going to search their houses and find the 'stuff', they would just dump the illegal stuff outside. If a dog touched a local, they would immediately wash themselves with sand and water. Seamus described an incident in a village:

> Whenever the dogs would arrive, the locals would gather out of curiosity to see such large dogs. One day in a village it was hot and dusty, so I took a swig out of a water bottle and then I cupped my hand under it, poured water into my hand, and Mick lapped it up. The reaction to this from the locals was one of horrified disbelief. But that was the good news. It went from bad to worse when I then drank again from the water bottle, even though Mick did not touch it, the locals went into gut-wrenching disgust at me.

The Australian commander at the time was Colonel (Col) Bill Mellor. He wanted a police dog presence in the massive embassy compound at Mogadishu to dissuade some infiltrators who were making a nuisance of themselves. The embassy compound housed a large number of foreign consuls-general and their staffs. Although the EDDs were not trained as security dogs, they were nonetheless big dogs with sharp teeth. So, the Royal New Zealand Air Force would fly the dogs from Baidoa to Mogadishu, a distance of about 300 kilometres, for the dogs to perform security duties, and they were successful in that role. It provided a happy reunion for the Australian dog handlers to catch up with their five US Marine mates who were housed in that compound. It also provided an opportunity for the dogs to visit the United States Army Veterinary Corps officer, Captain Steven Waters, who had his vet surgery there.

Back in Baidoa, the EDD teams supported 1 RAR infantry and 3/4 Cavalry Regiment armoured patrols at a place called Bahackabar, nicknamed 'Little Ayers Rock', because of its rock formations. The patrols would spend seven days there disrupting the movement of the insurgents across that part of the country. The insurgents eventually abandoned that area as a safe route for their movement.

On Australia Day 1993, all troops were invited into 3/4 Cavalry Regiment to receive two cans of beer to help celebrate the day. EDD Mick's name was on the nominal roll, so Seamus asked for Mick's ration of beer along with his own. The Cavalry Warrant Officer was not amused and asked where the dog was located. Seamus answered that he was back in the dog compound. The warrant officer knocked back Mick's beer ration on the grounds that he was not present to receive it. On ANZAC Day the same issue of beer was allowed. This time Seamus took Mick with him. Same warrant officer, but he still refused Mick his two beers. In disgust Seamus left, but in exercising Mick he allowed him to run off lead. Mick found the cavalry monument with its silver ensign of a scorpion, and its decoration for an ANZAC Day memorial service, cocked his leg and pissed all over the silver scorpion. There was an immediate reaction. The Cavalry guys wanted a piece of Seamus and his dog, but the Infantry guys warned them that if one hand was raised against the sapper or his dog, there was going to be big trouble sometime soon. Seamus and Mick escaped unscathed.

The tour of duty went for four and a half months and the drama about putting down the dogs rather than bringing them home became acute. There was a lot of public debate in the Australian media, including a cost-value exercise about the cost of training replacement dogs compared with paying for quarantine through the United Kingdom. The outcome was that the dogs were not put down and that Defence paid for the dogs to go through the full quarantine process before being admitted back into Australia.

The Australian EDD were helped significantly by the assistance of the US Veterinary Corps' Captain Waters, who reported that the dogs had been maintained at a high standard of veterinary care, and wrote a letter of commendation about the way in which the Australian soldiers had maintained their dogs' health and wellbeing. The dogs were transported to Kenya from Mogadishu with Darren Davis looking after them. They then went from Kenya to the UK, where they remained in quarantine for seven months. They travelled back to Australia and spent a further two months in quarantine at Eastern Creek in Sydney. Mick and Tia continued on as EDD in 3 CER under control of Seamus and Darren. Duke was gifted to an Australian Ordnance Corps female warrant officer because of age-related issues.

Back in Australia Seamus returned to 3 CER in Townsville and served out his time and was discharged from the ARA. Mick was re-teamed with Sapper Bob James who took Mick to Bougainville in the Solomon Islands during the conflict in that area. Tia also served in the Solomon Islands with Sapper Brendan Cook.

THE SOLOMON ISLANDS

Corporal David Simpson was section commander of the Explosive Detection Dog Section of 3 CER, based in Townsville. David has served on four overseas deployments, which include one deployment to East Timor in 1999 as an armoured personnel carrier driver, one deployment with EDD to the Solomon Islands in 2003 as the EDD Section 2 IC, and two deployments to Afghanistan as EDD Section Commander.

David was posted to the Solomon Islands in 2003 as the EDD Section 2 IC. There the aim of the EDD Section was to search the court house, prison cells and hotels to identify any objects that could be used by high-profile criminals as weapons or secondary missiles, and for any explosives that may have been concealed in those places.

The principal area in which David operated was around the capital, Honiara. One item which the EDD Section assisted in detecting was the uncovering of a shipping container full of Powergel, an explosive used in quarrying. This was removed from the container and destroyed by fire. It was not considered to be a cache of illicit explosives – just some old material that had been stored for too long in a shipping container. There were no other items of interest found during that tour of duty, but the EDD Section contributed to a sense of security in respect of Australian support to the Solomon Island authorities.

East Timor

Corporal David Wells,
Royal Australian Corps of Military Police

In 1989 David joined the Army Reserve (Ares). After attending his recruit course at Brighton Army Camp, Tasmania, he served with the 12th/40th Independent Rifle Company for about two years. In 1991, David was posted to 111th Combat Supply Platoon, then transferred to the Regular Army in June 1995. David was allocated to the Royal Australian Army Ordnance Corps (RAAOC) and posted to the 3 Brigade Townsville, where he served until 2000. David was promoted to corporal and posted to the 2nd Cavalry Regiment (2 Cav Regt) where he served as the acting B Squadron quartermaster sergeant.

David served his time and elected discharge from the ARA. He returned to Hobart and rejoined the Ares and was posted into the 111th Combat Supply Platoon. In 2003 the Corps transferred to the Ares Military Police (MP) unit and the same year rejoined the Regular Army.

In 2005, David was deployed to Iraq, where his job included personal protection duties for Australian diplomats and high-profile personnel. His team was responsible for protective security around the embassy compound and also when travelling through the red and green zones.

MP Dog Unit

David succeeded in transferring to the MWD stream. In 2007 he attended the basic dog training course at the MP School at Holsworthy near Sydney and was then posted to the MP Dog Platoon at Oakey in Queensland. David was teamed up with Military Police Dog (MPD) Maximus. After a period of continuation training, David and Maximus prepared for deployment to East Timor by joining the 3 RAR Battle Group, and conducting further training in both Sydney and Townsville. In 2008 David and Maximus, together with Corporal Jeremiah Gibb and his MPD Zac departed Darwin bound for East Timor. On arrival in Dili they were received by their MP compatriots and settled into the kennel area located at the heli-pod. Sergeant Dean Hedberg was the MP Defence liaison officer in charge of the dog detachment. The duties at the time included having dog teams on standby with the Quick Reaction Force, supporting the Australian and New Zealanders on their infantry patrols and providing general security duties for the heli-pod. The MP dog teams were often located with the Kiwis for a week at a time, on a rotational basis. The patrols included checking streets and roads as well as movement through the surrounding bush area in order to provide security for the locals against possible civil unrest. During the day patrols, the personnel were involved in 'meet-and-greet' activities with the local people. David's dog Maximus was not the most social of animals and the Timorese were apprehensive about large dogs, so David and Maximus would remain at a polite distance from the meet-and-greet activity. Things were totally different for night patrols, as David described:

The curfew commenced at 2200 hours and nobody was supposed to be on the streets after that time. This allowed the MP dogs to travel at the front of the patrol to give early warning should a person be breaking curfew and hiding in a dark area. However, the gangs of youths did not universally respect the curfew and the infantry patrols encountered them almost every night. Quite often we would patrol along a street or road and we would hear a commotion up ahead. As we would approach the group of people, they would be shouting and waving their arms about in an excited manner. We simply walked up to them and asked them to stop shouting and go home, and as the dog was out the front of the patrol, the Timorese would shy away and become more compliant with the directions being given by the patrol commander. The dogs were respected and most Timorese preferred not to become involved in confrontations with the security forces when dogs were present. This was handy during loud arguments or potential violence. The people would apologise and say things like 'yes sir, sorry sir' and then move off as directed.

David and Maximus served for six months in East Timor and returned to Australia in 2009.

The flight back was by chartered civil air from Dili to Darwin and then on to Sydney. The dogs were taken to the AQIS station at Eastern Creek where they remained for 30 days before being released back to duty with the MPD Platoon at Oakey. On return to work, newly returned personnel undergo a 'decompression' phase. This entails reporting for duty for half days during the first week of duty. During this time the soldier completes any medical and psychological matters that may need to be addressed. This is followed by a period of post-deployment leave; in David's case, he added another week of annual recreational leave to that to coincide his return to full duties with Maximus's return to the platoon.

Dave was promoted to sergeant in early 2010 and continued to serve with the MPD Platoon.

On 2 September 2010, Maximus succumbed to progressive degenerative disease in his hind quarter and was euthanised. Good boy, Maximus, you served our nation well.

Sergeant Dean Hedberg,
Royal Australian Corps of Military Police

Sergeant Dean Hedberg was born in Gympie, Queensland. He joined the Army Reserve when he was 17 and served with D Coy and A Coy, 9th Battalion Royal Queensland Regiment. In 1987 he was promoted to corporal and served as an Infantry Section Commander and later as Platoon Sergeant. In 2002, Dean was attracted to the Military Police because the MP had MWDs. On transfer into the Regular Army in 2002, Dean attended the basic MP course, which lasted for three months, and then asked for employment in the MPD stream. However, the personnel management policy was that he would need to serve for 12 months in a non-MPD posting before he would be considered for a change of trade stream into the dogs. Dean was posted to 1 MP Coy in Townsville in April 2002. During this posting he was deployed in September 2002 as a security attachment on far northern border security, returning to Australia in February 2003. In June 2005 Dean deployed to Malaysia and Singapore as a member of Rifle Company Butterworth as the MP attachment. At the end of 2005, he was successful in transiting to the MPD unit based at Oakey. In February 2006, Dean began his MP dog handler course and graduated in May of that year.

Two weeks after he graduated from the dog course, Dean was deployed to East Timor. He could not take his own dog, MPD Rutley, because of complications with the dog's rabies vaccination. So Dean was teamed up with a pool dog named MWD Beavis. The notice to move was very short. There was a five dog-team contingent told to stay close to the phone ready for immediate deployment. Dean's call came at 2300 hours when he was at home. He grabbed some gear and reported to the MPD Platoon at the Army Aviation Centre Oakey. At 0200 hours they enplaned at Oakey and flew to Townsville. From Townsville to Darwin they flew by civilian air charter and then by RAAF C130 transport aircraft from Darwin to Comoro airport near Dili in East Timor.

The situation in Dili was extremely tense. There were murders, riots, looting, house burnings and general civil unrest in many places. The local police were under extreme duress and needed assistance very quickly.

The C130 approach was tactical and when the MP diggers and their MPDs deplaned they were wearing body armour and their personal weapons were at 'action' (a bullet in the chamber ready to fire). They deplaned quickly, loaded their gear and dogs onto their Unimog truck and drove to the East Timor Police detention centre in Dili. It was now getting dark and they had to get set up as quickly as they could. The MP dog teams were to provide security for the detention centre and to support infantry patrols mounted by the 2nd and 3rd Battalion Royal Australian Regiment (2 RAR and 3 RAR). This demonstrated the flexibility of these dog teams. When they were assigned to detention centre duties they were required to act in the role of security dog teams for the facility; this included detaining a person with one bite to the forearm and holding them there until the arrival of a law-enforcement officer. When they were assigned to infantry patrols they provided a broad capability, and notably the ability to track humans, which included giving the patrol a passive alert to the presence of a person of interest on two entirely different missions.

MPD Rutley arrived in East Timor in July and Dean re-teamed with him. Beavis became a pool dog and was operated as a back-up for other MP dog teams. On one patrol, says Dean:

Rutley and I were called to a site in support of a 2 RAR patrol.

They had identified a dangerous person who was heavily involved in the illegal drug and weapons trade. The infantry wanted this guy urgently and MP Corporal Steve Wood and his dog Max and I with Rutley were briefed that the offender had bolted along a path. The offender was in such a rush to get away from the patrol that he lost a thong. Steve Wood and Max scented on that and followed up the offender, only to find the other thong on the path. This confirmed that Max was on the right track. The track lead to a village but night had come and we had to wait until the next day to continue the follow-up of the offender. His track led to a group of houses in the village and Max showed interest in one house. A search of the house revealed a cache of weapons, but the offender had bolted again.

This was a successful search in which the dog was the principal device for the success of the mission. The offender would have a lot more respect for the patrols knowing that dogs were never far away.

In another incident:

Rutley and I were called to the area near the Komoro Bridge in Dili, where another shooting had occurred. It was at night in an area well known for gang violence and marauding armed groups. We were given sketchy details of the shooter but enough for Rutley to pick up his scent. He tracked the offender despite the presence of people, chickens, detritus all over the place and the presence of the gangs of youths. Again my coverman was an AFP officer. Rutley tracked for about 45 minutes and ended up in a cluster of houses with animal yards including pig wallows and chicken coops, banana plants and fences. Rutley wanted to jump a fence in order to continue with the track. But that would have led us into more of the same thing and a possible ambush. We called the track off, but the AFP coverman and I were really happy with the way Rutley managed to hang onto the track. From my point of view, it was hard trying to read the dog in the dark wearing night-vision goggles and this was another reason why we called it quits when we did. I would not have been able to see Rutley indicate a potential ambush in the darkness.

Dean had a lot of confidence in his AFP coverman. The AFP policeman was in the Special Weapons and Tactics (SWAT) team in Australia. He knew how to react and he would have been totally reliable had things gone pear-shaped that night. In a third incident, Dean experienced an incident with armed civilians:

Rutley and I were working in the area of the Aqua Pod [A-Pod, a place where ships would come in] and we were told that a person had ridden up on a motorcycle, drawn out a pistol and shot dead one person and wounded two others. We were called to track the offender. After much deliberation about the details of the attacker and the direction of his escape, Rutley picked up the scent and we were off tracking. My cover man was an Australian Federal Police officer. It was early afternoon and the heat and humidity were fierce. Rutley tracked through streets and alleys but lost the track where the ground had been contaminated by people and vehicles.

Many times police officers and patrol members would be confronted by gangs of youths. The youths knew that the uniformed personnel would not open fire without extreme provocation. So they pushed their luck to a certain limit and would try to intimidate the patrol members to get them as far on edge as they could. Where a patrol was supported by a dog, the dog team would be placed at the rear of the patrol to add depth to the confrontation, but when the youths appeared to be inciting violence, the dogs would come to the front and the youths would become very compliant, very quickly. The youths also had metal darts which they would fire at the patrols using a bow and arrow technique. The darts, steel projectiles fired from sling shots, could cause serious injury. The chance of losing an eye to one of these devices was always present and injury to the dogs was always a danger to our mind, as they did not wear any protection against these weapons. Again, the dogs were used to disperse these youths into the adjacent alleys and pathways and away from the main streets or roads. There is no doubt that a dog the size of a German Shepherd demanded respect, and got it.

There was good cooperation between the RAAF MWD teams and the MP dog teams. The groups would assist each other when the need arose to add depth to a dog-oriented requirement. The AFP was deployed many times on building searches. They could initiate a building search on intelligence reports without the need to gain a search warrant first. The MP dog teams worked with the AFP Fast Reaction Teams throughout the city of Dili and surrounds. The patrol with the AFP became a regular task and was looked forward to by the MPD handlers due to the different nature of the work involved, which included building searches. All of the handlers developed a very close relationship with the AFP, which would ask for dog support quite often – this would cause some suspects to surrender without trying to hide in the buildings.

There was a strange twist to one incident. Dean and Bevis went on a mounted night patrol with 2 RAR on board an armoured personnel carrier. The patrol was moving down a road when they were overtaken by two locals on a motorcycle who were clearly quite drunk. For some reason the person driving the motorcycle lost control, which caused it to flip over its front wheel, throwing the pillion passenger onto the bitumen. He hit the road so hard that he broke his nose, lost teeth and managed to generally mess himself up. The Australians stopped, administered first aid and moved the unconscious civilian into the back of their vehicle. Gangs were roaming with their darts and it was not a good idea to be caught outside the personnel carrier in the middle of the night. The civilian was stabilised and taken the way to the hospital. On the journey he regained consciousness in the back of the vehicle, which was illuminated with red light. When he opened his eyes he was aware of being in a red environment and was looking straight into the panting face of Beavis. He must have thought that he had died and gone to hell.

In October 2006, after five months in-country, Dean and Rutley returned to Australia.

On his return, Dean resumed his job at the Military Police Dog Platoon at Oakey. In April 2008 Dean, now a sergeant, was required to deploy again to East Timor, together with MPD Rutley. Dean deployed with 3 RAR as the MP MPD detachment commander with three corporals with their dogs under his command.

On this deployment the gang violence had reduced, but the patrol activity was still intense. Dean's dog teams would move with 3 RAR patrols in both bush and urban settings and provide a tracking capability when required. During this deployment the United Nations management teams were taking over from the military and the UN preferred to keep the military to last resort.

The MP dog teams worked with the Kiwi Infantry and Kiwi Aviation (Iroquois) asset often. Dean discovered that the Kiwi

Aviation asset had a strange sense of humour. They had made a wheel of misfortune which worked like a chocolate wheel. The wheel would spin and stop at a segment where a message was written. The aim of the wheel was to choose a fate for a person who had made a bad mistake during the previous week, and the 'chocolate wheel of fate' was always bad news for its victim. The Kiwis asked if one of the segments could include 'Dog Attack', meaning that a victim would be attacked by an MPD. Dean agreed reluctantly, but with a host of safety procedures in place. Eventually a New Zealander managed to spin 'Dog Attack'. The problem was that he was a pilot – not the sort of person you would want to have all chewed up. Rutley was chosen as the dog to attack the Kiwi pilot. Dean prepared the pilot with as much dog attack protection as he could. Generallym when training a dog for 'man-work' the person would wear a training sleeve. The pilot donned this and was also wearing a video camera taped to his chest. Rutley went straight for his arm and gripped with his canines. The Kiwi pilot was looking a little red in the face with the effort of the dog on the arm, so Dean broke off the attack. The Kiwi pilot was shaken but not stirred – he sent the video footage to his mum in New Zealand. So grateful was his mothjer that her son had been treated so lightly that she sent over a box of Schmackos (dog treats) for Rutley. But it didn't end there. A second Kiwi spun 'Dog Attack' and Dean gave him the attack sleeve. However, this guy was a little different. He got dressed in a chicken suit and started to cluck and squawk when Rutley was ordered to attack the sleeve. Rutley didn't care whether it was a big chook or not, he saw the sleeve and took it in one massive, snarling bite. The Kiwi/chook came close to laying an egg. Dean returned to Australia in October 2008 and resumed his duties with Rutley at the Military Police Dog Platoon at Oakey.

Vietnam

Private Peter Haran,
Royal Australian Infantry

Peter was well under the age for overseas postings (19 years minimum age), but when the Tracking Wing was being raised at the Infantry Centre with a focus on tracking and dog handling, Peter was asked if he would like to train as a tracker dog handler. He did, and on arrival was teamed up with a dog named Caesar. In early 1967, he completed his tracker training and was posted to 2 RAR with Caesar. Posted at the same time were Denis 'Fergie' Ferguson and tracker dog Marcus. They were stationed at Enoggera in Brisbane.

In mid-1967, 2 RAR commenced its move to South Vietnam aboard RAAF transport aircraft. The advance party included Peter, Fergie, Caesar and Marcus. The requirement for the dog teams being in the advance party was so urgent that neither digger received their battle readiness training at the (then) Jungle Training Centre at Canungra in Queensland. This was an unusual situation.

The RAAF flew the 2 RAR advance party to Butterworth Air Force Base in Malaysia where the dogs received their inoculations, then on to Saigon in South Vietnam, before finally arriving at the 1st Australian Task Force (1 ATF) base at Nui Dat. There the dog teams were allocated an area which included well-constructed dog kennels with concrete runs, drainage, wash points, chain-wire enclosures and covered accommodation for each dog. Peter remarked that the Royal Australian Engineers had done a magnificent job of constructing the dog facility. The area where the tracker teams were housed was in the Support

Company (Spt Coy) lines which had, up until then, been the home of 6 RAR of the Battle of Long Tan fame.

Acclimatisation training in the Spt Coy rubber continued for about three weeks until the main party of 2 RAR, ex-HMAS *Sydney*, arrived. Very soon after, they were into combat operations in a serious way. This was June of 1967 and the tempo of operations was very active in Phouc Tuy province. As a result, the management of the dog teams had to be flexible. Both 2 RAR dog teams were placed on immediate standby for rapid movement should a rifle company contact the enemy and need a rapid follow-up tracking capability. To enable this, Peter and Caesar were in one dog team ready to go at short notice and Denis and Marcus were in another dog team. One dog team would deploy at any one time by helicopter straight to the hot spot, while the other would stand by at Nui Dat, ready for immediate deployment should another contact, in another rifle company, occur. The result of this was that the two teams never worked together in the whole time of their tour of duty. They would meet occasionally at a fire support base, but never out in the bush on tracking duties.

Peter remembers two tracking operations which were very testing for himself and Caesar. This is the first, in Peter's words:

The area known as the 'light green and the long green' was situated about 11 kilometres to the south-west of Nui Dat. This area had a notorious reputation for being festooned with large quantities of the M16 mine – also known as the 'jumping jack' because it would fly up about a metre into the air before it fired. The results of casualties from this mine were always horrific.

One day 12 Platoon of D Coy had been involved in a large contact with the enemy in the light green area. A dog team was called for. It was my turn, so I grabbed my combat gear, collected Caesar and went to the 2 RAR helicopter landing pad – codenamed 'Eagle Farm'. There were three of us: my coverman, a machine gunner, myself and of course, Caesar. We boarded a Huey (UH-1 Iroquois helicopter), took off, and within 10 minutes arrived at the D Coy position. We quickly deplaned and were taken to the contact site. There was a great deal of blood scattered on the sandy ground as well as streaked along some bushes. My coverman said, 'I'm ready when you are.' The platoon commander (who had been commanding 12 Pl for only one week) gave the order to commence the track. Caesar began his track at a fast pace and the tracking team followed at the end of his leash. 12 Pl did not patrol on the track; they were aware of the landmines and preferred to move off the sides of the track. My coverman and I had no choice but to honour where Caesar wanted to go, and he wanted to go on the track where the strongest enemy sign was. We patrolled for a couple of hundred metres, when we came upon a T junction in the track. This was a dangerous situation and I willed Caesar to point. He did not. Instead, Caesar came straight back to me and sat on my foot. He had never done this before. We were now stopped and exposed in the middle of an open track. The next thing, there was a terrible explosion and we discovered that the platoon commander had stepped on a mine. It exploded and blew off both his legs. An engineer splinter team arrived and began clearing the mine blast area with their counter-mine equipment. Once cleared the casualties were treated and evacuated by Dustoff medical helicopter. The two sappers then went in front of Peter and continued their sweep for mines along the track which lead to the T junction. At the T junction the sappers removed a large anti-tank mine and four M16 anti-personnel 'jumping jacks'. Caesar had never received any training in mine and explosive detection, but he was suspicious of what he found at the T junction and for good measure came back and sat on my foot so that I would not continue toward the danger. Soon after, we were all airlifted by helicopter back to our base at Nui Dat. That was the worst day I was to experience during my tour of duty. That day haunted me then, and continues to do so to this day.

But there was worse to come at that very place. This was the same T junction where, two years later, another infantry platoon would be cut to pieces by M16 mines. The incident was the inspiration for the haunting song 'Nineteen' by British musician Paul Hardcastle. The song has a strong anti-war message, focusing on America's involvement in the Vietnam War.

Peter was emotionally affected by the events of that operation. On his arrival back into the Spt Coy lines, he put Caesar away, went back to his tent and commenced maintaining his rifle. On reassembling the weapon, Peter lost concentration on what he was doing and accidentally fired a bullet. The round narrowly missed Denis Ferguson, who was sitting on the bed opposite Peter. Peter's commanding officer, Lieutenant Col 'Chicka' Charlesworth, gave Peter his field punishment. He had to fill and emplace a shedload of sandbags for the next two weeks, dressed in full combat gear, by day and night – watched by the 2 RAR Regimental Police. He managed to completely sandbag the dog kennels to protect them from shrapnel and blast effects from incoming enemy shells and mortar bombs. What the Regimental Police did not know was that Peter's mates would smuggle the odd can of beer to him using their superb tracking and camouflage techniques.

Operational duty continued out of Nui Dat on tracking missions until late 1967 when Operation Santa Fe was mounted in the north-east of Phuoc Tuy province. The purpose of the operation was to provide security to a large US Army Corps of Engineers group who were land clearing along the Firestone Trail. It was a big show which involved 2 RAR, 7 RAR, 3/5 US Cavalry and their Direct Support Artillery units and the US Engineers. The two Australian battalions were to sweep each side of the Firestone Trail and the Cavalry were to provide close protection to the Engineers. However, there was a big contact which hit the Engineers hard. There were serious American casualties. In Peter's words:

> We were in a fire support base when an urgent call came to provide a tracker team to support the Americans. A helicopter came for us and myself, Caesar and my coverman Bob Moodie were taken to the Firestone Trail and landed in the 3/5 US Cavalry area. The enemy had fired a number of RPG 7 rockets at the bulldozers and hit them. The enemy then did their usual 'bug out' back into incredibly thick jungle. The Cavalry carried us to the site of the contact and we were escorted by a group of American GIs who were armed with a wide assortment of weapons, wore military clothing of sorts and had a ferocious disposition to 'kick ass' when they closed with the enemy. At the site of the contact, we were shown plenty of enemy sign and told to get going.
>
> Our initial investigation confirmed that the enemy were a large group of Viet Cong (VC) reinforced with North Vietnamese Army (NVA) regulars. Caesar took the scent and we took off in pursuit of the enemy group. The jungle was really dark, but we had a small path to follow which the enemy had

used. The GIs took up an aggressive assault formation behind us and we pressed into the bush at tracking speed. As we penetrated deeper into the jungle we came across huge bomb craters, divisions of track into different directions, an assortment of vegetation types, and of course the heat and humidity. Caesar kept tracking the enemy despite the confusion of tracks. After several hundred metres, I was sweating and it was an effort to keep up with the dog.

Then Caesar pointed. I looked ahead at a bend in the track and saw the flash of bare skin of a man's arm and a patch of black uniform above it. They were 75 metres ahead. I told Bob 'there's the enemy' and he came forward with rifle in shoulder, gave the thumbs down (enemy sighted) to the Americans and they immediately and very quietly went into attack formation. I could then see at least three enemy soldiers standing in a clearing ahead. This was probably a campsite. I looked down at Bob's feet and saw a Claymore directional mine at his feet, but the detonator was out of the device and it could not be fired. Quite clearly, the enemy did not know that we were right behind them. Bob opened fire, the enemy responded and then the Americans 'hooked in'. There was a massive fire fight in which I needed to shoot a VC who was too close for comfort while at the same time keeping Caesar on a very tight lead because he was not happy with the enormous din that was going on around him. The Americans then launched their attack and swept the enemy away. Some VC/NVA bolted down the track, followed for a short while by the GIs. A VC/NVA officer was wounded and the American officer wanted to carry him back for questioning.

Bob advised that the VC/NVA would be back for a counter-attack and because we were a small group, now low on ammo, we should make a fast exit back to the Cavalry position. So we returned to the Cavalry as quickly as we could. When we arrived, we mounted quickly into the armoured personnel carriers and travelled back toward the American base camp. On the way back, we were attacked from a flank by enemy troops firing RPGs and small arms. The Cavalry had plenty of experience with these situations and immediately counter-attacked. An American trooper on one of the APCs was wounded and knocked down from his machine gun. Bob Moodie took over the gun and resumed firing. I was firing from the rear hatch of the APC and all the spent cartridges were falling over Caesar. I looked into his eyes and I can tell you, Caesar was really pissed off at me. We arrived back into the Cavalry base where we were treated to rock 'n' roll music, hot steaks and cases of beer. We stayed overnight with the Americans and next morning when we were about to be helicoptered out, they asked us to stay on and help them some more. But we had to go back to 2 RAR. It was the end of an absolutely textbook track, point and successful attack sequence of events.

Further tracker support to the infantry companies continued and the dog teams uncovered enemy, weapons and explosive caches, camp sites, bunkers and indicated on sign left behind by the enemy at places such as rivers and clearings in the jungle. The training received at the Tracker Wing was excellent preparation for their roles on operations in Phuoc Tuy province. The main problem was when Australian troops encountered the M16 mines. There was no answer to these as they proliferated everywhere and it was mainly pot luck if you actually saw one in the ground before you stood on it. It was tough work on a soldier's mind.

At the end of his tour of duty, Peter had to hand Caesar over to the incoming dog handler. This included obedience training and practice tracks inside the Nui Dat base. Then Peter said goodbye to Caesar for the last time and left Nui Dat. Peter returned to Australia and was posted to the Tracker Wing at the Infantry Centre. He was promoted to corporal and instructed on tracking skills and dog handling, but paid particular attention to the threat of mines and booby traps. Peter developed this training by laying out trip wires across a track, burying ordnance and laying an assortment of lethal items in and around the path of a track so that his handlers would be able to read a non-human detection response from their dogs. Peter remained at Tracker Wing for three years and was then posted to 3 RAR at Woodside in South Australia.

Caesar was retired to the Australian Embassy in Saigon in July 1970 where he became the absolute centre of attention of Jeremy and Sally White and their family. However, Caesar re-visited Peter in a most unusual way. At the 'Welcome Home Parade' in Sydney on Saturday 3 October 1987, Peter was gathered with a bunch of his mates after the march in the Phoenician Club. They had 'hooked into' the beer and were enjoying each other's company. Peter was touched on the back by an unidentifiable person and this person pushed something into Peter's hand with the words, 'This is for you.' Peter took the item to a chair and sat down to look at it. He found it hard to focus at first because it looked like a 20 cent piece. But then focus kicked in and Peter had a cathartic experience. The item was a silver identity disc and on it was engraved 'D6NO3 CAESAR'. His dog had returned to him.

Lance Corporal Brett Charlton,
Royal Australian Infantry
Lance Corporal Brett Charlton calls Northampton in Western

Australia his hometown. After leaving school, Brett worked in the bulk grain industry until he was 18 years of age and then, in 1966, joined the Regular Army. His father had served in the RAAF as a bomber pilot during WWII, his uncle had been a sailor in WWII and his grandfather had served in Europe as a soldier in WWI. Brett received his recruit training at the 1st Recruit Training Battalion at Kapooka in NSW and then his Initial Employment Training at the School of Infantry at Ingleburn in New South Wales.

As Brett was too young to be sent overseas, he was held at Ingleburn on the infantry tactics demonstration team. He found this boring and applied to become a tracker and dog handler. Brett was interviewed by Captain Barry French and Warrant Officer 'Blue' Carter and accepted on the course. He trained dogs, but many of them failed the gun shyness test.

In 1968 Brett was posted to the 1st Battalion, Royal Australian Regiment (1 RAR) which was in the process of replacing 7 RAR in South Vietnam. Brett moved to South Vietnam as a part of the 1 RAR advance group by Qantas air via Sydney, Singapore, Saigon and then to Nui Dat – the home of the 1st Australian Task Force.

On arrival at the 1 RAR location at Nui Dat, Brett was introduced to his dog, Justin. Justin's handler was tracker Private Tom Blackhurst (killed in action on his second tour of duty with the Australian Army Training Team). Justin was a Kelpie cross Labrador. On handing Justin over to Brett, Tom had to totally ignore the dog so that Brett could bond with him. Brett and Justin bonded quickly, which was just as well because three days after arrival in country Brett and Justin were called out for tracking duties. This occurred near the township of Hoa Long where an Australian-laid ambush was triggered and there were a number of enemy trails leading away to the west, in the direction of the Long Hai Hills. Brett learned very quickly that Justin was a brilliant tracker. He had an enthusiasm for the job and picked up human scents very quickly, and particularly if the scent was Viet Cong (VC). However, as the Australian patrol was crossing open ground, over what had once been old rice paddies, a spotter in an aircraft saw a group of VC form a firing line to engage the exposed Australian patrol. The track was aborted before the VC managed to bring effective fire on the Australians.

The work for a tracker team was often a short-notice affair. The team consisted of a tracker and his dog, a coverman (sometimes trained as a visual tracker) who was armed with a rifle, and a support digger who was often armed with an M60 General Purpose Machine Gun (GPMG). These three diggers were often called out at night and flown into a contact area. This happened when a night ambush had been triggered and there was strong evidence that some VC soldiers had escaped the ambush but were not far away. One of the humorous slogans used by the trackers was 'You lose 'em, we find 'em.' Next morning the tracker team would lead off to track down where the VC went.

The Battle of Fire Support Base Coral
On 12 May 1968, forward elements of 1 ATF flew into Fire Support Base (FSPB) Coral. The Australians were not able to fully set up and coordinate their defensive location before nightfall and the North Vietnamese Army (NVA) recognised this and took advantage of it. It should be noted that the NVA were regular soldiers, not the part-time 'shoot and scoot' local VC. In the early hours of 13 May 1968, the NVA attacked the Australians with overwhelming force. They overran the 1 RAR Mortar Platoon and temporarily captured their six 81mm mortars, captured

the Number Six 105mm Gun/Howitzer from 102 Battery of the Royal Australian Artillery, blew up the ammunition bay of Number One Gun and put loads of pressure on every unit and sub-unit that were in their way. By next morning the scene at FSPB Coral was one of devastation, death and clear evidence that a desperate battle had just barely been saved by the Australians. Included in the battle was 161 Battery of the Royal New Zealand Artillery.

Also included in the series of battleswere two tracker dog teams. This is the story of Brett and his dog Justin. In Brett's words:

We flew into the FSPB by helicopter and were ordered to set up next to a small dirt road. Our position had a road drain in it so myself, Justin and my coverman, John Quane, dug in and waited for orders. None came, so we waited. We were located with the HQ of 1 RAR. Then, in the early hours of 13 May 1968, all hell broke loose. We heard the NVA attacking with mortars, recoilless rifles, heavy machine guns, unending rifle fire from their AK 47s, the noise of whistles, bugles, shouting and lots of guiding tracer (green) to give them their direction of attack. Our diggers answered with the full force of everything we could possibly hurl at them, including support from helicopter gunships and 'Spooky' DC3 aircraft, together with some bombing missions from United States Air Force Phantom F4C aircraft. Huge flares turned night into day. The NVA seemed to be everywhere. They appeared to run over and passed us on their way to their own set objectives. It was a very dangerous situation to be in and we were very grateful when first light arrived and some relief came. Poor Justin hated the never-ending blasting and booming but remained under my control in the fire pit. The firing of my own rifle didn't help him much either.

In the morning, the remainder of the Task Force arrived, mainly by road, and began to construct defensive works with a great degree of urgency. The battlefield was like a scene from a surreal Hollywood set. There were numerous dead NVA soldiers lying on the ground, either singularly or in groups. Body parts and torn limbs and equipment were scattered over some areas of the battlefield. There were still some NVA close to the Australian position and there needed to be a number of clearing patrols mounted to get rid of them. One NVA medium machine gun had opened fire after dawn and this had to be dealt with quickly. A fighting patrol of Australian diggers was formed to attack the area where this machine gun was located. Brett and Justin were assigned to this patrol in case a rapid follow-up was needed. The patrol approached the machine-gun area using fire and movement: get up, run a few metres, get down and fire in support of your mates who were up and running forward, and then when they hit the ground, you get up and run and then go down again, and repeat the process again and again until you overrun the enemy. Justin handled this fire and movement task with zeal. 'Every time I got up and ran forward, Justin was right there at heel,' Brett says. 'I would go down and immediately so too would Justin. He seemed to understand the drill, although the noise of it all was not to his liking, but he handled it with resigned acceptance that this is what I wanted, and he just did as he was told.' There was a moment of repulsion that Brett has tried to erase from his memory, but it is still there:

Towards the end of the fire and movement, we were told that a United States Army Cobra gunship helicopter had the mission to fire on the NVA machine-gun position, and we should go down and hold where we were until after the Cobra mission. The

Cobra came and delivered an enormous amount of fire onto the NVA position. I looked at Justin and what I saw made me choke with nausea. Justin had come across a dead NVA corpse and was licking at the sticky ooze which had been blasted out of the dead soldier's head and eyes. I couldn't believe he would do that. But afterwards when I thought about it, to a dog, something dead on the ground is a free feed. It's just that the thought that it was a human being sickened me. The memory of it still does.

The NVA attacked 1 ATF positions numerous times and did not succeed in their bid to destroy the Australian forces both at FSPB Coral and its neighbouring position FSPB Balmoral.

Justin really did not need a free feed. His combat rations weren't bad. Dog food looked like hamburger patties and came in a 20-litre drum. The dogs loved them and Brett confesses that surplus dog 'hamburgers' were sometimes eaten by the handler. Brett reckons that they tasted better than some of the human United States Army combat rations.

After FSPB Coral, 1 RAR returned to the 1 ATF base at Nui Dat. During the battles of FSPB Coral, Brett had been promoted to lance corporal. As a break, he was sent to Saigon on guard duty for seven days without Justin. Justin went back to Nui Dat.

On Brett's return to Nui Dat, he received a welcome he would much rather forget. Justin had been formally charged with a number of military offences, including disorderly conduct by attacking a fellow canine and, of course, conduct to the prejudice of good order and military discipline in that Justin damaged and destroyed government property. Brett was to 'front up' on the charge with his dog Justin. The 1 RAR regimental sergeant major marched Brett and Justin into the commanding officer, Lieutenant Colonel Phillip Bennett (later to become the governor of Tasmania) to have the offences dealt with and the appropriate punishment handed down. Brett kissed goodbye to his still new and shiny lance corporal stripe and stood before his CO shaking in his boots. The CO found the dog guilty of all the offences and committed Justin to two weeks' confinement to kennels on half rations and no exercise. The 1 RAR Regimental Police made sure of this by mounting a continuous watch to make sure that Brett did not sneak extras to Justin during the night. Brett copped a boot in the arse for having such a wayward dog, but he managed to keep his lance corporal's stripe. Brett had to keep the kennel clean by collecting the dog shit and washing down the concrete. But the two weeks' punishment was reduced to one week because Brett and Justin were called out on a short-notice deployment in support of a rifle company in the bush.

A typical short-notice deployment occurred when a B Company ambush commanded by Major Barry French (the same French mentioned earlier) was triggered during the night. Brett and Justin were flown in by helicopter soon afterwards so that a follow up could be conducted at first light next morning. At that point it was apparent that the ambush had produced a number of fresh tracks and blood trails for the tracker team to follow. Justin took the scent quickly and took off as fast as he could on the scent left behind by the VC. Brett and his coverman kept up with Justin at the end of a 6-metre leash. Justin indicated on rest areas and equipment abandoned by the VC. When the B Company patrol came out of the jungle they had to traverse open country, which had a scattering of low bushes covering it. Justin went to air scenting and continued on tracking. But they had to stop when they came into the area of another Australian patrol. Visual contact was established between patrols and French asked them if they had seen the enemy group that had survived the previous night's ambush. They had not, but were now in on the hunt for them. Justin had indicated that a large group of VC were close by and Brett passed on the likely direction to Major French.

Major French flew Brett and Justin back to Nui Dat and handed the continuing search over to the other Australian patrol. Not long after Brett arrived back in his kennel area in 1 RAR, he was told that the other patrol had found the VC and a successful contact had been conducted without any Australian casualties. A job well done by the trackers, again.

At the completion of 1 RAR's tour of duty in South Vietnam in 1969, Brett had to hand Justin over to the next dog handler, Private Denis Rowlands of 5 RAR. This was a hard time for Brett because he had to ignore his four-legged mate while Justin formed a new bond with Denis. During this time Brett was assigned to road convoy protection duties, mounted in Land Rovers fitted with 106mm recoilless rifles, for vehicles plying between Phuoc Tuy province and the capital at Saigon. He then returned to Australia.

Justin continued to serve as a tracker dog in South Vietnam until his discharge in 1970. He was retired to the loving care of a civilian banker in Saigon. It is understood that Justin did suffer from battle noise problems, which became increasingly more difficult for him to manage as time went on. After his experience at FSPB Coral, that would not come as any surprise considering that those battles were the biggest and bloodiest of all the ones fought by Australian forces during the Vietnam War. Justin is well remembered for his energy, enthusiasm, mateship, efficiency and for saving many Australian lives.

KOREA

Private Lance Abbott's first posting was to the 3rd Battalion of the Royal Australian Regiment (3 RAR) in 1952, which was stationed in Japan. Shortly later, 3 RAR was sent to Korea and occupied the notorious Hill 355. While on this feature, Lance's platoon commander called him out to go down the hill to see if he could coax a runaway German Shepherd dog (in those days called Alsatians) back into the Australian lines. It was suspected that the dog belonged to the British Army and had become lost in the front lines. Lance saw the dog and was taken by its well-kept appearance. So he talked to it in a friendly way and then commanded the dog to follow him. It jumped up and ran up to Lance, who took it back to his company position. However, the dog could not stay in the lines and so was given to a Royal Army Veterinary Corps unit. Not long after this, a call went out for each battalion to contribute one digger for training with the Engineers as a dog handler. Lance was the automatic choice, given his experience with the lost dog. Lance received much of his dog handling training from Corporal George Gray of the Royal Australian Engineers (RAE) and a British Army sergeant who was a very knowledgeable and had experience handling dogs with the London Metropolitan Police. The dog teams were trained as infantry patrol dogs and most of their patrol duties were performed at night.

Several of the trenches were unoccupied at night and the Chinese or North Koreans would quietly infiltrate these trenches so that next morning there would be a battle to reoccupy them by the British units. The dog units would be tasked to give early warning of enemy approach and to ambush them when they attempted to enter the British trenches. Sometimes this would go on for most of the night. The dog was trained to point out the position of enemy soldiers, including enemy ambush positions. When the ceasefire began to take effect, the dog teams were required to continue with night patrols and Lance found himself supporting either Canadian or British Army units on the front line. He ended his tour of duty in 1953 and was posted to the School of Military Engineering (SME) near Sydney as a dog handler. He had to Corps transfer from RAR to RAE at which time his rank changed from private to sapper.

On arrival at the SME Lance found that they had started a dog section which was commanded by a warrant officer whose only experience with dogs was the breeding of toy-sized dogs as pets. Later an officer was appointed, but he had been self-taught using a British Army dog training pamphlet. The dogs were randomly recruited and generally were unwanted family pets. This situation did not suit Lance and he decided to take his discharge from the Army in 1954.

In 1956 Lance decided to join the RAAF and upon graduation he was sought after as a ground defence operative due to his Korean War and dog handling experience. He was posted to aid ground defence of the United States Air Force base at Ubon in Thailand. The problem there was that the local Communist guerrillas would wait in the jungle strip adjacent to the airfield where the aircraft were approaching to land. They would open fire at the slowly lumbering aircraft and scored many hits on them. Lance was a sergeant at that time, and his team had the job of tracking down these guerrillas in the jungle. He took his dog teams into the jungle and when the guerrillas saw the dogs, they vanished. They did not come back.

Lance saw service as an instructor at the RAAF Base at

Edinburgh in South Australia and after 12 years with the RAAF, he discharged in 1968.

MALAYA

Phil, aged 17 in 1952, graduated from recruits and was posted to the 2nd Battalion of the Royal Australian Regiment. The unit was mobilised for action in the Korean War but Phil could not go with them because he was under 19 years of age.

The ceasefire in Korea began in 1953, but tension on both sides was acute and a number of violations of the ceasefire agreement occurred. Phil, now a member of 1 RAR, arrived in Korea in March 1954 please to be at war at last. But bad luck was to follow. One night while he was guarding a stores train at a station in Korea, another soldier had an accidental discharge from his rifle and the round wounded Phil in the right shoulder.

Phil returned to Australia where he rejoined 2 RAR at Enoggera in 1955, just as the Malayan Emergency became a hot issue. The unit was battle-ready and sailed to Penang on the MV *Georgic*, arriving at Penang on 19 October 1955. This was to be a two-year posting. It was also the first time that Phil was introduced to his military working dogs.

Phil was a rifleman in an infantry section of B Company based near the township of Ana Kulim in Northern Malaya. During this time he became interested in becoming a dog handler after a group of handlers from the RAE asked for infantry volunteers to come forward and be trained in dog handling. The dogs were an 'engineer store', and as such, came under the control of RAE.

The person in charge of the dogs was Corporal George Gray and it was his responsibility to train and team up the dogs with their handlers. The HQ of dog training in Malaya was at the Jungle Training Centre at Kota Tinggi in the south of the country. George Gray, who had experience in Korea with mine-detecting dogs, conducted interviews with prospective dog handlers from 2 RAR and he selected Phil and Phil's mate, Cecil 'Honk' Crooks. They went to the 2nd Royal Army Veterinary Corps Dog Wing at Kota Tinggi for training.

Phil was teamed up with a German Shepherd named George. But George was very gun-shy and would even bark at thunder. George was unsuitable for infantry operations and so Phil was teamed up with Lawder. Lawder was a patrol dog and worked off-leash in front of an infantry patrol. Honk Crooks had a tracker dog named Tex. The patrol dog worked to the front of the patrol and on indicating something, the tracker dog would then go in, on-leash, and conduct a thorough search of the area or item of interest.

When Phil and Honk returned to B Coy they were employed on numerous patrols and were instrumental in detecting the location of camps, hides, caches and follow-ups on Communist (CT) movement through the jungle. Lawder and Tex earned their rations and were popular among the diggers.

The biggest contact in which Phil, Lawder, Honk and Tex were involved occurred early one morning when Phil and Honk were exercising their dogs. In Phil's words:

Honk and I were exercising our dogs just after dawn along this road when we heard an enormous amount of small-arms fire coming from a big contact about a mile ahead of us. We turned around and headed back to our base and were met by a scout car, which took us back to camp quickly. Our gear was always packed ready for immediate deployment into the jungle and we were off to support the unit, which was heavily engaged with the enemy. Apparently, a rubber plantation owner went into the bush and was ambushed by the Communists. He and his Malay Police Field Force security guards were killed and a truck, which carried raw latex rubber, was hit and set on fire. B Coy went in hot pursuit of the guerillas using us and a Sarawak ranger (a native Dyak or Iban visual tracker from Borneo). An Army aerial spotter in an Auster aircraft flew overhead and indicated where the guerillas were crossing a river up ahead, but because there was no communications between our radios, the pilot had to undertake some ingenious manoeuvres to alert us as to his information. The follow-up intensified and we went into tracking mode. Last light overtook our patrol and we set up a night harbour. Just on dusk a Communist water carrier walked straight into our position and he was wounded in the hand. He took off into the bush, but a couple of days later we tracked him down, and by then, gangrene had set into his wound and he was in a bad way. However, the noise of the contact alerted the Communist patrol and they managed to escape out of our patrol area.

But there was a strange sequel to this event. Phil continues:

During the contact with the water carrier, Honk grabbed for his rifle and dropped the pilot line attached to Tex. Tex took off after the guerilla and began to track him down without Honk behind him. Tex disappeared into the jungle. With night upon the patrol, Honk could not follow up and Tex did not come back. At the completion of our mission, the patrol returned to our base without Tex. As the days passed, hope for Tex's recovery faded. Then, after seven days, Tex ran into the base and was reunited with us. We were delighted and so relieved. Tex looked like he had been in a war zone all right. He had wild animal bite wounds, open cuts, abrasions, bruises, very lacerated pads, a number of large leeches on him and his ribs were sticking out of his rib cage from hunger. He was a mess. But he was alive, he survived the ordeal and went on working as a tracker dog.

Phil took Lawder to the British Army vets in Johor and while he was there a British officer asked him to work Lawder, for about six weeks, in support of the Ghurkha Rifles. After permission was granted, Phil and Lawder worked with the Ghurkhas. During this time, Lawder had a magnificent 'point'. He indicated accurately the presence of a CT patrol which was over one mile away. The Ghurkhas were so impressed with this that Phil ended up with a Ghurkha batman to look after him. After this, Phil and Lawder were often called out in support of the police and other law enforcement agencies. Lawder indicated on many caches, stores dumps and camps used by the CT during their attachment to non-Army authorities. The one drawback was that the Malay Police Field Force was mainly Muslim. Phil had a food dixie for himself and another for his dog, and of course he slept with his dog. He was therefore considered 'unclean'.

In 1957, Phil was posted back to Australia and on his return he had to hand Lawder over to the engineers at Kota Tinggi. It was an emotional farewell given that Lawder had been such a useful combat multiplier to the Australian and other forces. Phil went back to Malaya with 1 RAR from 1959 to 1961 as a digger in the anti-tank platoon, but could not locate Lawder.

Phil discharged from the Army on 7 April 1970 and worked in government and security companies until he retired. On 5 March 2009, the commanding officer of 2 CER formed up his unit for his explosive detecting dogs to receive their medals. At the end of the parade, Private Daniel's name was called. He answered with a soldier-like 'Sir' and then fronted up on the 2 CER parade. He received the Canine Service Medal and the War Dog Operational Medal in recognition of the great work contributed by his dog, Lawder. It did take 42 years to come, but at long last, Lawder's work had been recognised in a manner befitting that of a good soldier. There were tears in Phil's eyes.

Afghanistan

Corporal John Cannon,
Royal Australian Engineers
John joined the Regular Army on 24 October 1990. He was allotted to the Royal Australian Infantry (RA Inf) and was posted to 3 RAR. There he qualified as a military parachutist (paratrooper) and after four years he had several other combat skill qualifications, including 81mm mortarman. As part of 3 RAR, he went to the RAAF Base at Butterworth in Malaysia for three months.

John always wanted to be an EDD handler in RAE but found it difficult to go to Engineers in 1990/91 because of the Gulf War. Almost every soldier graduating from Recruit Training was allotted to the Infantry at that time. After five years with 3 RAR, John decided to Corps transfer to RAE with the aim of being an EDD handler. However, on arrival in the Liverpool area, John was employed assisting the physical training instructors (PTIs) with maintenance of the swimming pool at Holsworthy. He became a PTI himself and spent a further six years in that location.

It took 13 years, but John finally completed his EDD course at the SME in 2003. This was followed by a posting to the Incident Response Regiment (IRR) in the Sydney area and then on to 1 CER in Darwin.

While at IRR, John was warned for overseas deployment. He and Sapper Phil Grazier were given one week to get themselves organised for a deployment to Afghanistan. This was in response to a call from Special Operations Task Group 1 (SOTG 1), already in Afghanistan, for the presence of EDDs to support their operations. The aim was to subject the EDDs to a trial and assess their usefulness in combat operations in that Area of Operations (AO).

The first two dogs which arrived in-country for this assessment were EDD Sam (John's dog) and EDD Jasmine (Phil's dog). Sam and Jasmine performed so well that EDD teams became an ongoing requirement in the initial search for illicit explosives, caches, ammunition and other items of interest to coalition units in the area.

The EDD dog teams were transported by Long Range Patrol Vehicles (LRPV) to places such as vulnerable points or river crossings, where they would get off the LRPV and search the immediate area for IEDs. One pass the coalition vehicles would traverse was littered with the debris of wrecked Russian vehicles, which had come to their demise in this location. The EDD team would work through and around the wreckage, searching for IED before proceeding through this defile. The EDD teams lead from the front protected by friendly forces on the flank. John remembers this location as being a place of immediate danger that needed to be approached very carefully. It was definitely a case of 'follow the sapper (and his dog)'.

Later search techniques with the Reconstruction Task Force (RTF) and the Mentoring and Reconstruction Task Forces deployments allowed the EDD to support an Engineer section of sappers who had mine detectors and other detection devices. But in the early days, it was the EDD teams that lead the way. John's team detected seven caches and this convinced the SOTG 1 command element that EDDs were worthwhile combat assets in Afghanistan. They have been there ever since. John's 3 RAR experience was well utilised at that time in that he often used his infantry skills to augment SOTG personnel when the situation called for it. John was instrumental in ensuring that all sappers arriving in-country to work in the EDD stream were also well trained in infantry minor tactics as well.

John and Phil remained in Afghanistan when SOTG 1 rotated out of country and joined SOTG 2 when it arrived. Although the normal deployment was intended to be about four months in-country, John and Phil served for six months on their first deployment. This was mainly due to the need to train the newly arrived sappers into the job. A part of the training problem was that explosives cannot be left in the ground without piquet in Australia. However, in Afghanistan, John could bury the ordnance in protected areas for weeks ahead of the time it was to be used as EDD search targets. This allowed the explosive scent to coalesce with the surrounding soil and set up a more operational search scent picture than was available to EDD trainers in Australia.

EDD Sam and EDD Jasmine were working so well it was decided to leave them in Afghanistan and to re-team them with the reinforcement sappers on the next rotation. In John's words:

I found this part of the deployment really hard. I knew that Sam had to be re-teamed with his new handler, which meant that I had to ignore him and show him no affection. He had been one of my closest mates and had worked so very well in the rough stuff, and now here I was treating him with indifference. Poor Sam didn't understand this and I felt so bad about it, I found myself weeping with grief for the little bloke. I boarded the C130 for my outward journey without a decent word of goodbye for him.

EDD Sam and EDD Jasmine worked for a further four months after John and Phil left Afghanistan before it was their turn to return to Australia. When they got back, Sam and Jasmine went through the quarantine system under the AQIS protocols in the Sydney area, and then resumed work as EDD in IRR. Here they proved to be excellent training media in the development of EDD skills for EDD handlers. They were retired on age from service six months later. They were both over ten years old when they retired.

An Urgent New Approach to Training EDD teams in Australia

In June 2006, John returned to IRR near Sydney. When he was posted to SME as an instructor in January 2007 in the EDD stream, he saw the need to update the training to accommodate the operational requirements for Afghanistan. The EDD training at SME was based on a program designed for a Northern Ireland situation. John influenced a shift of focus to Afghanistan. John travelled to 1 CER in Darwin just before that unit sent EDD teams to Afghanistan in support of the Reconstruction Task Force (RTF) projects. His presentations on the EDD search requirement for Afghanistan assisted in orienting the sappers with an environmental, tactical and explosive detection situation which, at the time, were ground breaking. This included the need to train the EDD around pungent human and animal smells and other conflicting scents in a search situation. John achieved this by coordinating the EDD teams into country showgrounds just after a rural show had finished. The stimuli (explosives, caches, ammunition etc) were hidden or buried in among the faecal matter of cows, chicken, horses and other animals. This exposure helped the dogs to work through the distractions of other animals' urine and faeces.

During his time at SME, John completed his supervisor and dog training courses. He trained up five dogs for EDD duties, but of those, only one dog, EDD Storm, successfully met all the criteria required for an operational EDD. John teamed up with Storm and they have been a team ever since. In 2008, John and Storm were posted to 1 CER in Darwin. John was promoted to corporal in 2007, and became the commander of the 1 Combat Engineer Regiments Explosive Detection Dog Section.

Second Overseas Service
On 19 September 2008, John and Sapper Troy 'Strawbs' Croton departed 1 CER for Afghanistan in support of RTF 1 at Tarin Kowt in Oruzgan province. Another member of John's EDD section, Sapper Brett 'Turls' Turley arrived ten days later.

The patrol base out of which the Australian EDD teams operated was nicknamed 'Camp Holland'. This base supported a number of forward patrol bases and John's team gave search support to RTF 1 elements on roads, vulnerable points and special areas. Most of the patrols were completed as one-day events, but many included overnight stays in a village or in the bush outside the safety of a patrol base. John and EDD Storm had a find in a cave system, which was the result of coincidence. John had laid some stimuli in a few caves for Storm to find. But

Storm kept indicating in an area where John knew he had not laid a target. After a couple of confirmatory responses, John realised that Storm had detected something that needed further investigation. Storm had found a fuse from an American aerial bomb. The Taliban had stored the fuse for future use in one of the caves, and Storm and John recovered it before it could do any damage to coalition troops.

In another find, John and Storm operated in an abandoned village and on searching a house came across a small animal compound where the floor was covered in straw. Storm paid a lot of interest to the area covered in straw and when John investigated he uncovered a false floor. The Explosive Ordnance Detection technicians were called and they subjected the area to an intensive search. They captured explosives, mines and ammunition, including mortar rounds, all stored under the false floor. This was a big find and Storm was given an extra pat for his efforts.

John and Storm were travelling in a Bushmaster armoured protected vehicle when it ran over an IED. The IED had explosives which had suffered some degeneration and the consequent blast only inflicted minor damage to the vehicle. There were no casualties and the vehicle remained serviceable.

In another IED incident, the vehicle and its personnel were not so lucky. A loud explosion had been reported and John's team were directed to drive there and render assistance if necessary. Another Bushmaster had driven into the area where the explosion had been heard and they knew that this was trouble. In John's words:

We arrived in the area where the explosion had occurred and stopped short over a rise to where we knew the stricken vehicle was located. I searched with Storm and as we came over the hill, I saw the vehicle and it was pretty messy. On nearing the stricken vehicle I could see that both front wheels had been blown off, the remote-control machine gun had been dislodged and there was other damage to the protective plates on the exterior of the vehicle. I knew that one of my EDD teams was aboard. It was Sapper Brett Turley and his dog EDD Gus. I was relieved to know that Brett and Gus had been evacuated by helicopter before I arrived. They were treated at an American hospital in Kandahar and returned to full duty three or four days later. The worst casualty was an Australian trooper with a broken leg. The Bushmaster can take a hell of a beating and still protect its passengers.

Contacts with the Taliban were mainly at long range and not very frequent during RTF 1 and in the early part of RTF 2. In winter the temperature was in the minus degrees, but low temperatures did not significantly affect the dogs. They were able to grow and thicken their coats for the extreme cold then shed the winter coats when the warmer weather arrived. In fact, Storm went for a swim in a stream where the water made its way around blocks of solid ice. John believes if Storm had not been castrated, he may not have been that keen to swim in winter.

In base, the EDD were housed in kennels, although these were very spartan. They could wear a protective oilskin style of dog coat, but were not afforded heated accommodation. There was contact with an American EDD handler who often visited the Australian EDD section. He was very motivated and the Australians nicknamed him 'Nacho'. Nacho and the Australian teams would lay stimuli for each other to detect and then exchange ideas on each other's techniques.

The deployment lasted nine months and John and his dog teams rotated out of Afghanistan on 25 June 2009. John escorted all the EDDs to the quarantine establishment in the Sydney area and returned to 1 Combat Engineer Regiment, and home, a short while later.

Part of John's responsibilities was to maintain records of every veterinary treatment for every EDD, including worming, daily medications, cuts, bruises and any visits to the veterinary team provided by the United States Army Veterinary Corps. The dogs had the fur on one front leg constantly shaved, just above the vein, in case an urgent fluid drip needed to be inserted. The USVC had a computer program for every dog in-country, storing the details of the dog in case they needed hospitalisation and urgent veterinary treatment. A printout of each dog's particulars was carried by the handler as a ready view to assist a medic when working out how much morphine to administer should a serious wound be suffered by the dog in the field. It was handy for administering medications as well.

John wants to continue in the Army in the EDD stream. He has deployed with SOTG and Mentoring and Reconstruction Task Forces, served with the Incident Response Regiment and has been an instructor at School of Military Engineering. Having served on operations with Special Forces, and as a combat engineer on conventional operations, he believes that he still has a lot to offer the ADF. He is keen to refine the process for the acquisition and training of EDD dogs.

5.

RAAF

In compiling this chapter I would like to acknowledge the assistance of the RAAF Dog Handlers Association, retired and serving members of the RAAF dog trade. Many individuals have shaped the Air Force MWD role and direction; even today staff continue to develop and adapt the role to ongoing RAAF requirements.

The Royal Australian Air Force has utilised dogs since WWII. Dogs were first introduced into the RAAF during 1943 when untrained and extremely savage dogs were placed loose inside warehouses and compounds, tied to aircraft or fixed to long lines in such a manner that they could run back and forth. Later, patrol dogs were used by the RAAF security guards to patrol vital assets of a base. They numbered in excess of 300 before numbers were reduced in order to meet government mandate financial targets, and somewhat fewer are employed today. Handlers have moved from part-time handlers with primary tasks elsewhere in the RAAF to the professional group that prevails today. Modern-day handlers are capable of being employed in a widely changing environment to meet the needs of the modern defence force.

Today, the RAAF is the largest single corporate user of

military working dogs in Australia. Its approximate 195 MWDs have an important role in the security of high-value RAAF assets at some 12 bases and establishments located across Australia. The RAAF currently has about 180 trained dog handlers on active duty. The next largest Defence Force operator is the Australian Army.

By 2010 over 2000 dog teams have graduated from the RAAF Security and Fire School at RAAF Base Amberley. Up until recent times the MWD training school qualified the Royal Australian Corps of Military Police, the Australian Naval Police and RAAF Security Police members. Today the Royal Australian Corps of Military Police train their own dogs and the Navy no longer employs dogs.

Traditionally the RAAF employed 'police' dogs for the sole purpose of security. While this type of dog could track using 'wind' scent, it was generally aggressive to strangers and predominantly used on foot patrols, alone, out of hours, on the flight line. Although reasonably effective in a benign security environment, these dogs were not considered suitable for use in ground defence operations. In 1996 a project team was formed to assess the capability of MWDs, in particular, working with Air Defence Guards in the Patrol and Surveillance Area (PSA), Close Approach Area (CAA) and Close Defence Area (CDA).

Bill Perrett is the man credited with the formation and development of the RAAF Police Dog Handler mustering. It was largely through his efforts that the first dog handler courses were conducted. He arrived in Sydney as a telegraphist aboard a British Navy ship at the end of WWII. In the early 1950s Bill was placed in charge of looking after the dogs used for the security of RAAF warehouses. He fought for recognition and acceptance of dog teams as an effective security measure and was assigned the responsibility of developing the guidelines and curriculum for a course. As this new mustering grew, the nickname 'Doggie' became synonymous with all personnel who became members. This term was, and still is, accepted proudly by members past and present. Bill became a commissioned RAAF police officer in the mid 1960s and was appointed the first officer in charge of the new Police Dog Training Centre at No. 7 Stores Depot, Toowoomba, Queensland.

Warrant Officer Robert (Bob) Jennings, who joined the RAAF in 1977, was one such student who attended the dog training course in Toowoomba. On graduation Bob and his dog PD Hobo, were posted to RAAF Base Fairbairn in Canberra. On completing their posting of two years, Bob and Hobo were posted to Singapore. The RAAF took over areas of this base after the Royal Air Force had departed and handed the base over to the Republic of Singapore Air Force. There were areas where Australian security interests required Australian surveillance and protective measures, such as Mirage and F111 aircraft. The Australian flight line was exclusively patrolled, at night, by a RAAF security dog and handler. In those days, the handler was armed with a Browning 9mm pistol and 20 rounds of ammunition, had no radio and no immediate backup. His area of responsibility included the flight line, headquarters buildings and any mission critical sheds that were nominated for security purposes.

In 1994 the Police Dog Handler mustering underwent a further change and became amalgamated into the RAAF Police mustering, with all handlers being renamed RAAF Police (RAAFPOL). In 1997 dog handlers, Police and Police investigators were mustered under the name RAAF Security Police. Dog handlers now become RAAF Security Police with the annotation 'MWDS' for Military Working Dog Specialists.

With the advent of modern warfare, the role of the dog handler changed to reflect the dog's specialist capability in a new security role. Belgian and German Shepherds are the breeds of choice and their training gives the RAAF the benefit of having man/dog security teams capable of seeking out an enemy before it can damage vital assets. Advanced tracking, combat troop support, tarmac protection and booby trap detection are all part of the MWDS duties. With the training and capability of working in all terrain from heavy scrub to urban areas, these dogs and the new breed of handler will lead the Australian Defence Forces into the new millennium.

The RAAF Security Police work with MWDs to provide security at RAAF bases. Their working environments can vary from modern air bases located near state capital cities to bare bases in remote regions of Australia. During their career, the MWD handlers and their dogs could also be deployed to foreign locations such as recent missions to the Solomon Islands, the Middle East and East Timor.

DRUG DOG DETECTION THROUGH THE ROYAL AUSTRALIAN AIR FORCE

The RAAF introduced a drug detection capability in a formal and official capacity in 1983. However, mention should be made of the work during the 1970s of a number of dedicated non commissioned officers who trained their allocated Police dogs to detect a limited range of drugs. This was undertaken through their own dedication and interest to develop further the role of a RAAF Police dog and with little or no official assistance.

The official development of an Air Force drug dog detection

capability came about in the 1980s through an agreement between the RAAF and Australian Customs Service (ACS) to train four RAAF NCOs and supply them with a trained drug dog ready to commence work at selected bases within Australia. The choice of Customs was simple in that the organisation is the Australian leader in training dogs to detect drugs through their Drug Detector Dog Unit based in Canberra.

The four NCOs to undertake the first RAAF sponsored ACS course were Corporal W (Billy) Manning, Corporal M (Mike) Newson, Corporal P (Skip) Lee, and Corporal W (Bill) Whyte. On completion of this course they each returned to their bases to work as a single man/dog team with the internal RAAF Police Service. Their efforts targeted on-base facilities and occasional special operations with local civilian police forces. As part of ongoing follow-up training each man/dog team was also able to work with their regional ACS operational drug detection dog units.

These teams continued for a further four years as a single independent unit until the formation of a mobile four-man team based in Sydney under the control of Sergeant C (Chris) Burgess in 1987. This unit functioned successfully until the advent of improved technology and random testing became more viable options.

Along with the new technological ideas and what can only be called a 'head in the sand' mentality, the RAAF decided that having drug dogs might give the wrong image to the public, and suggest that the RAAF had a drug problem. This same naive outlook caused information leakage prior to detection dogs arriving on a base, ensuring that if there were ever any drugs in the first place they would be disposed of before the team's arrival. This just proved to the 'bean counters' that since statistics showed no positive results, the expense of maintaining these dogs was unnecessary. The net result caused the RAAF to withdraw these MWD specialists from service.

One area that cause all MWDs to suffer is that their deterrent and success value cannot always be measured. Since their very presence deter trespassers and would-be offenders commanders often do not realise just how valuable an asset they are until they are not there.

Scout dogs were introduced into the RAAF during the late 1970s with handlers being drawn from the mustering of Airfield Defence Guard (ADG). These dogs and handlers were trained at the RAAF Police Dog Training Centre primarily for ambush detection duties while patrolling in hostile territory, usually outside base perimeters. Their secondary role was as outpost static guards. RAAF Airfield Defence Squadrons stopped having their own teams in the 1980s but after East Timor MWDs teams were spoken so highly of by many senior staff the ADG management community wanted to take over responsibility for the MWD muster. Bob Jennings agreed to help with that and moved from Amberley to the 2nd Airfield Defence Squadron (2 AFDS) to help write up the capability, all the supporting documents and aide-mémoires to establish the MWD muster in the ADG. Today MWD teams are supplied by RAAF Security Police attached to Air Defence Wing as required.

MWDs are now a well-established force multiplier: one dog equals a dozen men within the Australian Defence Force. In 2008 the RAAF celebrated 50 years of MWD training and they have played an essential role in the security of air bases since their formal introduction in 1958. Today MWD handler responsibilities incorporate a number of roles. Duties include providing policing and physical security as well as after-hours policing and immediate response tasks, along with advanced tracker skills used operationally overseas. MWDs also provide a man-trailing capability in support of ground defence operations, specifically scouting and clearing patrols for the Airfield Defence Guards (ADG). The standard work routine of a MWDH includes shift work patrolling the tarmac and associated tasks in line with that duty. These tasks could include arrest of felons and assisting general duties service police in their job, similarly to how a civilian police dog handler supports his comrades. However, there are certain responsibilities that working with a MWD entails. It is the duty of each handler to look after his or her own dog and to ensure that each MWD in the kennels is given an appropriate level of husbandry during his or her shift, and that they are adequately fed, groomed, washed and medicated.

Far from decreasing in numbers in the age of advanced technology, MWD are on the increase in all major military powers. Over recent years coalition forces have increased dramatically their use of MWD in the fight against terrorism. Explosive detection dogs are particularly in high demand and the RAAF established their own EDD teams separate from the Australian Army for use around their bases. The EDD capability of the RAAF is increasing with another EDD course run by the Australian Customs Department completed in 2011. The RAAF has also sent EDD handlers to the United States Air Force Training Centre in Lackland, Texas, for six month attachments. Handlers learn the latest EDD techniques and return to Australia with fully trained dogs from that course. Likewise, a number of EDD handlers in 2011 attended the Defence Animal Centre in the United Kingdom and undertook a similar course there.

The purpose of peacetime RAAF patrols is to:

- maintain discipline
- prevent and detect offences
- provide a protective security presence and response capability for ADF assets
- supervise access control (not personnel).

All of these functions form the peacetime role of the MWD handler, with the most important of these being to 'provide a protective security presence and response capability for ADF assets' under a force protection umbrella. These tasks are carried out by safeguarding ADF equipment, classified matter buildings and installations against theft, damage or destruction by sabotage, by working with a MWD as either a foot patrol or mobile patrol team.

The purpose of contingency or war patrols is to:

- support ground defence elements during ground defence operations
- detect enemy and follow to source
- detect caches and hiding up places
- detect entry and exit points of a mobile enemy
- assist in establishing clear ground for friendly forces.

All of these tasks are important during contingency operations. However, the most important of these is to 'support ground defence elements during ground defence operations', and through this support the other associated tasks. These tasks are carried out in unison with the patrol lead scout to safeguard ground defence elements against attack, working with a MWD trained to use wind- and ground-borne odour to detect enemy presence. To be employed in ground defence operations, the handler requires skills in basic ground defence tactics. Regardless of modern technology, the RAAF still regard dogs as the best way to patrol forward operational bases, particularly at night, and to search large amounts of vehicles at vehicle control checkpoints with EDDs.

The RAAF also supply fully trained dogs to Special Forces (SF) in operational areas such as Afghanistan. The Special Forces supply a small number of members to be trained as handlers while in-situ. They are trained and supervised by RAAF cap badge members but used in the field by the SF operators. As the MWDs are fully trained, there is only a need for a short handler operators' course to be taught to Special Forces, and the attached RAAF personnel are from the RAAF Police and Security mustering – there is a tight selection process for working for these units.

An area where the RAAF can benefit Special Forces operations is in the training of escape and evasion techniques. Escape and evasion from military dogs is a major concern to SFs who operate behind enemy lines and tend to work around facilities which are guarded by military security dogs. If located, the SF team may have to escape on foot to avoid capture. RAAF air crew benefit greatly from this instruction too because, if shot down behind enemy lines, their escape may require them to avoid enemy canines.

MWD Reserves
Not many people will be aware that within 23 Squadron (City of Brisbane), a RAAF Reserve Squadron operates a RAAF Security Police Reserve MWD element. In fact there are now Reserve MWD elements on most RAAF bases. Most current members of the Reserve MWD Flight have been permanent Air Force dog handlers prior to becoming Reserves. This is due to the MWD

course covering a training period of over three months; thus, a great deal of commitment is required of a reserve; in addition, each handler must commit to several days per month conducting security operations.

One exception to this rule was Bevan Case, who became a reserve MWDH, and was the first reserve dog handler not to have come from the permanent Air Force.

In May 2004 he commenced a 13-week RAAF MWDH course as a reservist dog handler. Bevan's prior experience explains how and why he was able to do complete the course. Bevan started as a Prison Dog Handler operating a GP Dog/Active Alert drug dog. In September 2000 he became the president of the Police and Services Canine Association Queensland. In 2009 he completed a further 12 week prison PAD dog course. Finally in 2010 he competed in the Australian Service Dog Association (ASDA) trials in Ararat, Victoria, with PAD Dog Ace and came second in narcotic detection work and third overall for detection work. He was also nominated as vice-president of ASDA. Bevan states:

> Having undertaken both the prison GP Dog course and the RAAF MWDH course, I wouldn't be able to say that one was far superior over the other. But what I did find was that certain aspects within the individual courses were better. For example, Prisons I believe had the better method of training and deploying operational in relation to building searches, while the RAAF man-trailing and how they approached the whole theoretical aspects and the steps taken to teach dogs and handlers to trail were better demonstrated and understood through the RAAF course.
>
> The other big benefit I found is that by having a foot in each

organisation I have been able to organise and undertake joint training days together on a semi-regular basis a lot smoother than had previously been occurring.

My RAAF reserve shifts are obviously dependent upon my Corrective Services shifts but I believe they contribute, as reserves have back-filled gaps in the roster which has then allowed PAF members to train, take short leave and attend courses. As an experienced handler I try and provide input and direction to some of the junior members but by also bringing my views from a different dog related environment in how we do business may also help handlers in situations that they may face in their military career.

Several of the Reserve dog handlers are also employed in the support role, conducting kennel management, training and breeding management roles.

Members of the Reserve MWD Flight have been deployed to operations in East Timor and are frequently deployed to both Army and RAAF bases to assist with security operations and training. Reserve MWD handlers can also be attached to the RAAF Air Defence Guard Wing, where they are employed as scout/tracker dog teams to Airfield Defence Guard operations. MWD teams are also employed to support RAAF Reserve Air Protection Flight (APF) in patrolling Base facilities.

History of RAAF Dogs

1943   First employed as savage guard dogs in compounds and tied to aircraft.

1954   Trained dogs and handlers operating as a foot patrol.

1954 Aug. Police Dog Training Centre opened at No. 2 Central Reserve, RAAF Albury, NSW.

1955 Dec. Centre moved to No. 11 Stores Depot, RAAF Tottenham, Victoria. Dogs used were various breeds and handlers were from various musterings.

1958   Decision made to use the German Shepherd as the sole breed for training as a police dog.

1962   The Security Guard mustering commenced with 22 handlers completing No. 1 Security Guard course in December and posted to Stores Depots.

1969   Police Dog Training Centre relocated to No. 7 Stores Depot, Toowoomba, Queensland.

1982   The Defence and Security Training School (DSTS) formed at RAAF Amberley with the primary task of training Airfield Defence Guard, Royal Australian Air Force Police, Fire Fighters and eventually Police Dog Handlers.

1983   A team of four corporal handlers selected for training as Drug Dog Handlers at the Customs Dog Unit, Canberra.

1986   Security Guards were renamed Police Dog Handlers.

1987	DSTS becomes the RAAF Security and Fire School (RAAFSFS) and Police Dog Training Centre relocated to Amberley under RAAFSFS. ̄
1988	The RAAF Drug Dog Operational and Training Cell established at No. 2 Stores Depot, Regents Park, NSW.
1994 Apr.	Police Dog Handlers and Police Investigators are amalgamated with RAAFPOL.
1996	The first Police Dog Handlers from the RAAFPOL mustering undergo training.
1996	The RAAFPOL mustering is renamed Security Police and a new badge is struck and approved.
1997	Police Dogs are renamed Military Working Dogs. A MWD-Rejuvenation Project Team is established at RAAFSFS to redefine the nature of the role and improve the capability for the long term. The Belgian Shepherd Malinois is trained for military purposes.
1999	MWDH training commences, introducing a contingency role supporting ground defence elements during ground defence operations. Public Service MWD Developers commenced work at RAAFSFS. The Timber Shepherd is introduced for assessment as a military working dog.
1999	MWDHs and MWDs are involved in peace-keeping duties in East Timor. This duty is continuing in conjunction with the Army
2001	The capability is endorsed by Chief of the Air Force.

2002	Public Service MWD Breeding Manager commenced work at RAAFSFS.
2001	Dog breeding trial is approved and instigated.
2003	Redevelopment of RAAFSFS MWD precedent in designated trailing breeding, development and foster care cells. Establishment of 156 kennels and day yards.
2004	RAAF Puppy Foster Care Program revised (The foster team program was introduced (MWD-RPT Project teams) and dogs first fostered out in 1996.)
2004	Full kennel cleaning contractors employed at RAAFSFS.
2005	Special Operations Command training of dogs and handlers for special operations. Four handlers and dogs graduated after an initial eight week course.
2006	Three RAAF support staff members posted to Special Operations Command (SOCOM) to maintain continuation training of dogs.
2006	Public Service MWD Supply Manager position created at RAAFSFS.
2006	Firearms and Explosives Detection Dog (FEDD) training commenced under Headquarters Combat Support Group by Australian Customs Dog Training.
2008	FEDD capability approved.

It is easy to focus on operations and conflicts MWDs have been involved in, but there are many other aspects to the job. Many service personnel, including myself, have spent the best part of their military careers in patrol bases ensuring the RAAF assets are secure. This is the thin blue line – the members who do the job night after night when all other RAAF personnel are sound asleep. The peacetime roles of the RAAF are varied, and include dog demonstrations for school groups and regular exercises to test the operational air power capabilities of the RAAF.

The RAAF MWD teams are often seen conducting public demonstrations from school visits to major tournaments. These demonstrations are used by recruiting staff as a tool to promote the RAAF and also help bring attention to military dogs in the services. Unlike their British counterpart, the Royal Air Force, the RAAF do not have a full-time dog demonstration team; instead, most RAAF dog teams are capable of putting on a display. They can achieve this due to their high standards of obedience and agility taught to them on their basic course. Even though these displays look spectacular to the general public – with dogs jumping through burning hoops, scaling walls, crawling under logs and balancing on top of a ladder – they all have an operational meaning and reason. Just like military police and their civilian police counterparts, in the course of their patrol duties RAAF teams will come across offenders who try to flee. Dogs are thus trained to jump fences, jump through windowss or crawl under fences in the pursuit of that offender. In a combat role these MWDs may have to scale battlefield objects under gunfire. All this is simulated on an agility course.

Exercise Pitch Black, the RAAF's largest exercise, is conducted on a bi-annual basis in the Northern Territory and Western Australia and is one of several exercises MWD teams attend. It provides an important opportunity for the men and women of the RAAF to train with multinational forces, including air force representatives from France, Singapore, Thailand, the

United Kingdom and the USA. Security Police and MWDs of 321 Expeditionary Combat Support Squadron,maintain night patrols throughout the exercise.

THE SOLOMON ISLANDS

In January 2004, Corporal David Skeels, RAAF dog handler was, deployed to the Solomon Islands for four months as part of the Regional Assistance Mission Solomon Islands (RAMSI) for a physical security role without his MWD. During the first weeks of this deployment, a New Zealand Air Force Security dog handler had to return home for compassionate reasons, leaving his allocated New Zealand MWD in the Solomon Islands without a qualified handler. An agreement was reached between local Royal Australian Air Force/Royal New Zealand Air Force (RAAF/RNZAF) commanders and Corporal Skeels was then teamed with the Kiwi MWD called Rocky for the duration of the deployment. The combined RAAF/RNZAF MWD team conducted the following roles: security of RAMSI aircraft assets and personnel; security patrols of Honiara Airport and the surrounding area, and providing a psychological deterrent in the international terminal during the arrival and departure of civilian passenger flights. In the Solomons RAAF dog handlers were part of a mixed security team consisting of RAAF Security Police and Air Defence Guards commanded by an officer. Their task was to provide security for Henderson Airfield, from where Australian planes operated.

EAST TIMOR

RAAF MWD handlers have been involved in operations in East Timor since the very beginning in 1999–2000 in Operation Warden and Operation Stabilise or INTERFET (International Forces East Timor, a multinational peacekeeping taskforce, mandated by the United Nations to address the humanitarian and security crisis), then in 2006 in Operation Astute, which was the same operation in 2008 and continues to this day. On October 1999 the RAAF's Security Police MWDs made their first overseas operational deployment during Operation Stabilise in East Timor. The eight RAAF members disembarked from a C130 at Dili's Komoro Airport. These MWDs were to play a significant role in the restoration of order in the country.

The detachment was headed by Warrant Officer Bob Jennings and consisted of eight MWD handlers, including James Ingram, Andy Floor and Sam Evans.

Whereas the vast majority of INTERFET personnel passed through Komoro Airport en route to every corner of East Timor, the RAAF MWD section were already in their own patch, tasked to support the Airfield Defence Guards (ADG) of No. 2 Airfield Defence Squadron in their efforts to maintain a secure airhead into Dili. It was the first time RAAF dog teams were deployed into an active operational environment. The deployment to Dili had two aims. Firstly, the dogs' presence with their capabilities for man-trailing/tracking, attack work and crowd control provided a very flexible asset for the commanders tasked with area security. The presence of the dogs also signified the ADF commitment to keeping peace around one of INTERFETs main point of entry – airfields.

Both ADGs and the attached MWD teams were to prove very effective over the next five months. Within two days of setting up a temporary camp adjacent to 3 Squadron Royal New Zealand Air Force, the MWD detachment received their first tasking, when 381 Expeditionary Combat Support Squadron (381 ESS) asked for MWD support to patrol ESS area – it seemed that some of the remaining Indonesian Air Force (TNI-AU) personnel were wandering through the area at night and were paying particular attention to tents occupied by females.

MWD patrols were soon present, often in pairs and demonstrating their attack skills as a high-profile way of telling the Indonesians to keep out. At the same time the section had its first encounter with East Timorese. Some of the returning locals had taken it upon themselves to cross the main airstrip at their own pleasure. After seeing the dogs in company with ADGs, they soon realised the error of their ways and within a short time such incursions dwindled to zero.

After four days in temporary settings, the MWD detachment moved into their own area adjacent to the 2 AFDS HQ. After taking over an abandoned house and making the necessary adjustments, the handlers began settling into the serious side of airfield security.

The dog teams were soon busy deployed on a wide variety of tasks, from providing forward scouting capabilities to the ADG patrols operating around Komoro to conducting security sweeps inside the Komoro Airport perimeter.

The MWD drew first blood when a TNI PUKSUS (Indonesian Air Force Special Troops) soldier got a little too close to MWD Rocky and his handler Leading Aircraftman Mick Gregory. Once more the TNI found good cause to look at the dogs with respect, not to mention caution.

As well as direct airport security, the dog teams were also tasked with keeping the gathering crowds of returning refugees from getting too rowdy. Other tasks included security for the Australian prime minister's aircraft when John Howard flew into East Timor and sporadic patrols of the Dili port compound to combat the rise in pilfering. All tasks kept the dogs busy and raised their profile.

The excellent relationship between MWD teams and the ADGs was to really come of age in East Timor. Although many ADGs had worked together with dogs in Australia on exercises, not everyone had done so. This proved not to be a problem as the ADGs had always been quick to recognise the value of having a MWD team alongside their patrols.

Each MWD handler carried full frontline ammunition, as did the rest of the ADGs patrol, and on night operations were equipped with NINOX NVG systems (night viewing aids). Extra water was also carried for the dogs.

Eventually, the combined ADG/MWD patrols had a significant impact on the morale of the local East Timorese. After just a few encounters with the Australian patrols the locals came to realise the RAAF were serious about keeping the peace in their backyard and would not tolerate any kind of trouble. To a population emerging from 25 years of occupation, this was a welcome way of learning that not all soldiers were brutal. This and the allied presence of the MWDs made the locals feel secure and sleep a little more soundly at night.

On patrol the MWD teams would encounter a multitude of sights and sounds. In addition to walking up front with the scout and keeping an eye on things up there, the handlers also had to look out for the safety of their dogs. The kampongs around the airport were full of stray mongrels that, as time went on, became more willing to take on the MWDs. Handlers could not take the chance of their dogs being bitten by one of these disease-ridden mutts so the ADGs soon sent them packing. Other risks included snakes, scorpions, heatstroke and on one occasion a stray pig put the wind up MWD and handler while on night patrol.

When not out on patrol, daily routine for the dog teams included getting rest and personal admininstration. The dogs were checked daily for parasites and given any necessary veterinary treatment. Like soldiers, dogs have to undergo constant training to maintain their skills. Each dog was put through some form of daily training such as tracking or attack work to ensure that they remained switched on.

The dogs were housed in a set of temporary kennel frames that were flown in from Australia and set up under cover to allow for maximum protection from the elements. These kennels were washed out daily and the faeces burned. Rations for the MWDs were often supplemented by catering staff from many INTERFET units, who tried to throw some meat our way whenever they could.

The handlers themselves were also responsible for the upkeep of the MWD section. With the resourcefulness and humour for which all Doggies are known, the MWD building grew from a stripped-down hut to a well-constructed complex that was the envy of all who saw it.

The RAAF MWD handlers have also been conducting joint operations in East Timor, including Operation Tanager/Operation Citadel, which involved attachments to 3 RAR from 18 April 2002 to 22 October 2002. They consisted of four man-dog teams (three RAAF and two Army) to support battalion strength, stretched out across East Timor. There were two types of patrols: blue hat patrols, for which we wore the blue UN hats to win the heart and minds of the local population; and the green patrols, which consisted of going out on patrol on the border to locate militia and Indonesian soldiers.

The dog teams were used as early warning detection devices using both airborne scent (the wind) and ground-borne scent (tracking/man trailing). They could also carry out building and area searches, apprehend the enemy, crowd control and be used as force multipliers.

The teams were normally attached to a forward observation post on the border and would go out on patrol in full sections (ten men), half sections (five men), and with sniper and reconnaissance teams. These patrols would spend up to five days out on patrol away from base, carrying their own food and water and all the supplies for their dogs. A lot of the patrols were in the mountainous regions, which was tough going – a kilometre could take two hours. This type of terrain often required the teams to drop their packs and crawl through lantana.

In the patrols the teams normally acted as forward scouts for early detection and when in a harbour up position they would use the dogs' capability to secure the position and alert to any approaching enemy forces. They were also used to detect crossings on the border where the militia and Indonesian National Armed Forces (TNI) would cross to raid villages.

In December an additional five MWD teams arrived from Australia to boost manning and help to cope with the extra tasks that had been taken on. By this time 2 AFDS had replaced 5/7 RAR on security duties at the heliport in Dili and a MWD team presence was also required there.

The dogs proved as big a hit at the helipad as they had at Komoro. Soon many members of the heliport contingent were going up to ask about the dogs' welfare and again to offer extra rations. The MWD were considered a morale booster, providing a lost link with pets back home. East Timor provided an ideal platform to spread the gospel of MWD operations. They also demonstrated to the Army how valuable tracker dogs could be and what a great force multiplier they are (at this stage the Army did not have this capability).

While all of this was going on, the business of patrol/ security ops was continuing as normal. In December MWD teams Ingram, MWD Kelly and Evans and MWD Bear were called to a scene of confrontation next to Komoro bridge where a returning family was being accused of being militia by a large local crowd. Within ten minutes of arriving at the scene the 300-strong crowd had effectively been broken up, much to the relief of 5/7 RAR and 2 AFDS. This incident highlighted the flexibility of the MWD detachment and further generated interest among the INTERFET and civilian police forces. This multinational peacekeeping taskforcetook notice of the use of dogs in such theatres. The incident also gained the respect of the locals who had to reassess the 2 AFDS presence in and around Komoro.

By January 2000 the original eight MWD teams had began to be rotated out and new replacements from Australia deployed. The new teams continued the patrol/tasking pattern that had been set and also commenced patrols of the rowdy Dili market area as a means of keeping the peace.

Confrontation with the East Timorese continued as local gangs tried to take advantage of the law and order void that was bound to occur as the nation began to rebuild itself. One such incident was encountered by MWD team Newcomb and MWD Tyler who had to quell a violent crowd with a well-placed '42 tooth exchange'. One of the great advantages of MWDs is their use as a non-lethal force option.

The second contingent of MWD teams served on in the country until the withdrawal of 2 AFDS, which was replaced by Portuguese troops in late Febuary. The Portuguese, who expressed a high level of interest in the work of the ADFs dog teams, have MWDs in both their air force and elite paratroop battalions.

By March 2000 the last RAAF MWD teams had returned to Australia where each dog was placed in quarantine at Eastern Creek, Sydney. Sadly, during this period of quarantine, the only deployment loss occurred when MWD Prince was diagnosed with *Brucellosis canis*, an infectious bug found in East Timor. Prince had to be euthenased.

It was not the last time MWDs would be deployed to East Timor. Within two months of the last teams' return, the call came for them again, such was the reputation of a job well done.

Again in 2006, Sergeant Shane Campbell and MWD Rex and Corporal Jason Thompson and MWD Lex were the first two MWD teams 'in-country'. They flew in on the second aircraft to Timor on the night of 25 May, landing at approximately 2300 hours.

Within hours of arrival, over 6000 refugees were at the airport seeking protection. Due to 'priority taskings' of aircraft, determined by Army movers, Jason and Shane were the only two MWD teams in country for the first three days of operations as other MWD teams, standing by in Darwin, kept getting bumped from aircraft to aircraft. They should have been on the third aircraft in. The next arrival of MWDs were most welcome because the first teams had been up and working from 0500 hours on 25 May, pretty much non-stop for three days.

Today, MWD with Timor-Leste Aviation Group Operation Cell provide security for Black Hawk helicopters and are on standby at all times for base security. They maintain a constant patrolling program from dusk to dawn, with their trusty four-legged friends. Operation Astute is the Australian Government's response to a request from the Timor-Leste's government to assist in restoring peace to their country. The Australian Defence Force has deployed to Timor-Leste with a mission to assist the country's government and the United Nations to bring stability, security and confidence to the Timorese and allow them to resolve their differences democratically and peacefully. At the time of writing, there are approximately a thousand ADF personnel currently serving in Timor-Leste. This force will remain there, continuing to provide a robust response capability to support the government and the UN Police force.

There is an issue about final separation from service of a MWD from the RAAF which needs some attention in the future. In a letter from the President, ADFTWDA, to the Vice Chief of the ADF in September 2011, the following concerns were raised:

That RAAF MWDs separate from service via a hypodermic syringe. Euthanasia. There is evidence to suggest that this is an extreme measure, which is causing resentment and frustration with handlers. There are many RAAF MWD handlers who believe that their dog has the capacity to adopt civil standards of behaviour, in a family home, when the MWD is at the end of its operational service life. It seems ironic that the RAAF led the way in this area some years ago, and now appears to be the only service not to adopt the initiative.

The Military Police assess their MWDs against a criteria for suitability to adopt civil standards of behaviour when they are discharged from the Army. Those which satisfy these criteria are released into the civilian community. Army engineers do not have a problem with their dogs because they are all passive (non-aggressive) animals.

The RAAF may face another change in the near future, with the advent of the Force Protection concept and additional security requirements set by the USA for the protection of aircraft newly acquired from them. Naturally, as we have seen throughout the RAAF's history, the Doggies will adapt and rise to the challenge.

In both civilian and military environments these scenting and man skills that MWD teams bring to a commander is their ability to save human life. These skills should not be discounted when developing planning for operations.

Warrant Officer P.J. Andersen
SECPOL2MWDH
RAAF, Australia

This poem by Grant Teeboon, currently serving in the RAAF, is an example of a handler's bond to his four-legged mate.

Why I became a Police Dog Handler

A torch & a radio hang off my belt
In winter I freeze, in summer I melt.
I'm awake all night, I'm asleep all day,
Will I patrol my life away?

Ours is to see, and not to be seen,
That black & tan shepherd with the handler in green.
If you don't see us, the man or the dog,
Rest assured we're doing our job.

Those long conversations where nothing is said,
Where he lifts his paw & I pat his head.
He gets all the attention, and deservedly so,
He's the most courageous creature I know.

He'll sit, down or stay, or rip off your legs,
One word from his handler, and he'll tear you to shreds.
When he brings down a man, his tail will be wagging,
Though seldom in anger, more likely just bragging.

My big furry playmate, so fearsome & tough,
And I'll never tell you how much is bluff.
All that excitement by the light of the moon,
We've waited for months, it's all over too soon.

This same old patrol is becoming a habit,
The only excitement, a cat or a rabbit.
From sunburn to frostbite, from mozzies to flies,
To the wind in your face and the sun in your eyes.

We've braved all the elements to make piles of money,
The piles I've got, and the pay just ain't funny.
So why you may ask do I favour this life,
Where I talk more to 'him' than I do to the wife.

If it isn't the pay, the perks or conditions,
Then what is the reason for this silly rendition?
The reason I stay here, and the reason I slog,
Is not for the money, but for the love of a dog.

So why, you may ask when you quiz,
Is the friendship between us so fine,
Because the life he lays down will be his,
And the life that he saves will be mine.

6.

NAVAL POLICE DOGS

A fire at Naval Air Station (NAS) Nowra in December 1976 completely destroyed a hangar and numerous Tracker aircraft, leading the Office of the Navy to recognise the need to upgrade security at the base. In early 1977 police dogs were introduced to the Air Station. Initially Police dogs and handlers from the RAAF were used, and the first Naval Police and Police Dog team took up duties in July 1979.

The German Shepherd was preferred by the RAN to other breeds because of its physical attributes, intelligence, dependability, versatility and receptiveness of training. The Belgian Shepherd was not chosen because of the ill-founded belief that the dog is savage. Indeed, neither a savage nor a timid dog is accepted for training. The RAN does not breed its own MWDs but relies on the RAAF for its supply of dogs. Only pure breed Shepherds of either sex are accepted.

As in all services, the careful selection of people suitable for training as handlers is vital to the successful employment of Police dogs in the RAN. At all stages of training and operational use, the handler and his dog work as a team, often with the minimum of supervision, therefore the selection of suitable personnel for training was no less important than the careful selection of dogs. Not only does the Naval Police handler have to cope with the training of his dog, study dog psychology and dog husbandry, he must also be conversant with normal Naval Police Practice and Procedure and can be called upon to carry out any Naval Police duties. Handlers are selected from all ranks of the Naval Police. They must be a volunteer for dog duties, their Naval Police Task book must be completed and they must be assessed as suitable for dog handling duties.

The training of the handler and his dog is carried out simultaneously at the RAAF Police Dog Training Centre, Queensland. The handler and his dog are initially trained in obedience work. This means that the dog is taught to obey commands given by the handler in a series of repetitive habit-forming exercises. The dog must learn to do as he is told before he can be expected to succeed with further training.

The training is then advanced to developing the dog's natural agility. The object is to ensure that the dog learns to surmount all obstacles within its physical capabilities. Several of the obstacles encountered during this training are hurdles of varying heights, a tunnel, a vertical scaling board, a ladder, a log walk and a fire hoop. These are all based on obstacles a MWD may encounter during patrol operations.

After success in obedience and obstacle training, the dog is trained in attack work. The object of this training is to ensure that the dog is capable of detecting the presence of an intruder or criminal by wind-borne or ground scent, chasing and apprehending an escaping intruder, defending his handler and/ or himself against attack and disarming an intruder or criminal armed with a firearm or other weapon, as well as guarding and escorting these persons after apprehension. The dog is also trained to be unafraid of gunfire.

At the end of the training course the handler and his dog are posted to NAS Nowra where they will start their new life working together.

What's required in the way of security on Naval establishments in peacetime Australia is a matter for debate. The threat of sabotage or vandalism sometimes seems remote and the deterrent value that the Naval MWDs have played cannot be measured. The RAAF, who have had Police dogs for over 20 years state that a handler-dog team is equivalent to a dozen guards on foot patrol. The inherent abilities of German Shepherds complement the effectiveness of their human handlers. The dog will alert the presence of someone, and the handler is then in a position to decide how to handle the situation, either by awaiting reinforcements before making a move, or solving the situation by challenging the person and unleashing the dog to hold the intruder for questioning or search. Although a closed-circuit television system could be used in well-lit areas, such as for a line of parked aircraft, TV cameras cannot smell or detect small sounds and there is no guarantee that the viewer is going to be looking in the right place at the right time, or sufficiently alert to notice the flicker of movement which could mean a threat to property. Police dogs represent good value for Navy dollars invested in security. The RAN decided to do without MWDs to protect its shore-based assets in the 1990s and no longer uses them. My belief is that this is backward thinking. Given terrorist attacks on US Naval ships and assets recently, let's hope it does not take another incident for the Australian Navy to again decide to use these proven security assets.

7.

MILITARY POLICE
WORKING DOGS

Military Police provide commanders with an essential element of command and control through the application of the four main Military Police functions of law enforcement; mobility and manoeuvre support; security, and internment and detention operations.

The Military Police law enforcement role is a critical component of the military justice system in both Australia and overseas. While on operations, the 1st Military Police Battalion provides law enforcement and administers international civilian law. On the battlefield the Military Police provide commanders with an essential element of mobility and manoeuvre support, conducting route reconnaissance, route signing, controlling and monitoring traffic movement, controlling military stragglers and the movement of the civilian population. Military Police provide support to logistic operations and also physical and personal security. Within the specialist roles of the Military Police are the Military Police Dog handlers who are responsible for the training, husbandry and handling of the MPDs used to detect human intrusion, track people, act as a deterrent in crowd control and apprehend personnel suspected of committing criminal offences in peace- and war-time environments.

The first Army Police Dog section was formed in 1977. The purpose of this unit was to maintain a high level of security for the Army Aviation Centre in Queensland. Oakey Aviation Centre, 30 kilometres west of Toowoomba, is a high-security level facility not just because of the current climate of terrorist threats but because it is also the home of the Army's latest and sophisticated helicopter assets, a role which continues to this day. It was known as the Base Support Squadron Police Dog Unit, and boasted a posted strength of five dog teams. The members were all volunteers, and came from various Corps.

MPDs underwent many changes over the next decade including several name changes. Members were still recruited from all Corps, and retained whatever pay level they had previously been allocated. In 1990 the unit was given a singular identity when they were incorporated into the Royal Australian Corps of Military Police (RACMP). Incorporation into the RACMP meant all members received the same pay level, and opened both career progression and posting opportunities. Today they are called the MP Dog Platoon, Delta Company 1 MP Battalion.

The next major change to occur was the introduction of a new training doctrine, which saw the phasing out of police dog training, and the commencement of MWD training.

MWD Handler Responsibilities.
MWD handlers provide a number of roles within policing and physical security. Their duties also include after-hours policing and immediate response tasks. They also provide a man-trailing

capability in support of ground defence operations, specifically scouting and clearing patrols.

The MP/MWD Platoon maintains a state-of-the-art kennel facility where MWDs are individually housed on concert floors with raised bedding and full shade. The kennels are specially designed so that each dog cannot see its neighbour to prevent agitating each other. Like all MWDs, each dog believes he and his alpha human partner are the kingpins of the kennel, not the rival canine and its handler 'pack' next door. Music is piped throughout the kennels for behavioural enrichment and there is a separate quarantine kennel facility for the housing of new recruits and MWDs returned from operations.

Unlike many law enforcement canine units where the handlers take their dogs home every night, the Army keep their MWDs in the kennel facilities. There are several large grass runs by the kennel area which provide the means for the dogs to run about while off duty.

Next to the kennels is the agility course, which incorporates simulated walls, tunnels, windows, ladders, long jumps and various obstacles designed to train the dogs as they are likely to encounter such obstacles during operations.

To become a Military Police MWD handler is not an easy process. Firstly, you have to be accepted into the Military Police Corps, which can be a difficult and challenging process in itself. Once there, you must spend at least 12 months performing general MP duties before applying for specialisation as a MWD handler. There is a rigorous selection process (there are always more applicants than positions available) when applicants are tested on their suitability to become a handler. New handlers undergo an intensive 16-week initial basic MWD course, then a further 12 months of development training prior to being eligible for full operational status. Training is continuous with regular exercises and weekly sessions.

The operational duties are wide and varied. Primarily, the role is security but due to the flexibility and professionalism of the dog teams the Army hierarchy have rediscovered the reconnaissance capabilities of MWDs as demonstrated during their deployment to the Solomon Islands and East Timor. Like their civilian counterparts, MP/MWDs can be used in riot control situations and are an ideal force multiplier with large crowds. In the garrison duty role they can likewise be used to effectively apprehend criminals with no lethal force (apart from 42 very sharp teeth), track down offenders or search for missing persons. This flexible platoon also has an on-call search and rescue (SAR) response, primarily for the Army aviation assets in case of a downed or lost aircraft. Like all defence units, with aid to civil power procedures in place they can also be used to assist in civilian SAR operations.

The current peacetime role of the unit is to provide:

- specialist information unit commanders
- discipline and morale within the Army Aviation Centre
- maintenance of law and order
- Vital Asset Protection/key point security (aircraft, airfields, defence installations and the like), prevention of unauthorised removal of classified material
- Defence Aid to the civil community and agencies
- Defence Force Aid to the civil power
- search and rescue capability
- VIP protection
- security of visiting forces' aircraft.

The war-time role incorporates all of the above, with additional responsibilities including:

- early warning at traffic control posts (TCPs)
- building searches
- movement and detention of prisoners of war
- special operations
- support to ADF (Infantry assisting with listening posts, clearing patrols and the pursuit of fleeing enemy).

In May 2011 I attended the graduation course of students and was highly impressed; the Military Police dog teams have come a long way since I conducted a course with a member of the MP predecessors unit, the Army Aviation dog team, in 1981. These dogs showed great control and instead of the usual display of a dog attacking a bloke dressed in a padded suit, these dogs conducted a realistic display of the type of role they will no doubt come across. MP/MWDs jumped through windows and door access points to attack various armed offenders inside a building. With smoke and battle noise plus friendly forces also in the room, it was more akin to an SAS hostage take down display in a 'killing house', a special building where tactical scenarios using weapons are practised.

Australian Military Police Dog handlers attached to the International Stabilization Force regularly take their canine friends on ANZAC patrols in and around the streets of suburban Dili. Military Police dogs and their handlers are a highly valued asset in peacekeeping operations.

Police from Australia and 24 other nations throughout the world provide security in Dili. The ADF provides support to these police operations as required. The New Zealand Defence

Force (NZDF) is working alongside the ADF to assist with this mission.

One recent role of the MP/MWDs in East Timor was being employed by 4 RAR in conjunction with reconnaissance teams, leading Infantry through jungle terrain in search of infiltration points. The presence of the MWD team proved to be very popular and provided a high level of comfort to those involved because the canines superior sensory powers were invaluable in the early detection and in the deterrent role.

In the Solomon Islands the Military Police MWDs were involved in security, crowd control and general police canine deterrent roles. The MP/MWD teams were used by international UN police agencies in the execution of high-risk warrants and prisoner transport protection. In fact, when there was a dangerous offender involved, the MP/MWD were called for support. This was because the local police have no dogs of their own, plus traditionally dogs or the fear of them is ingrained in local traditions, causing the police dogs to be much feared. This was a good thing as often a dangerous situation would quickly de-escalate once a dog arrived on scene. The Military Police MWD teams were required to respond to these emergencies at short notice. One way of achieving rapid deployment to trouble spots around the island was by helicopter insertion.

8.

SPECIAL FORCES

While the images in the book were graciously provided by Defence Media, the Australian Defence Force implies no endorsement and/ or agreement with the information contained within. Thus, accounts and/or representations of Special Forces activities are to be considered the author's opinion. I have deliberately left out some information, such as names and places, for security reasons. The resulting relatively short chapter underlies the very real and dangerous job these canine handlers do.

The Incident Response Regiment (IRR) is an Australian regiment that is part of the Special Operations Command. Its mission is to provide specialist response to incidents involving chemical, biological and radiological (CBR) and/or explosive hazards, including other hazardous materials and situations including fire. The Incident Response Regiment is based on the Joint Incident Response Unit (JIRU) that was established in 2000 as part of the Australian Defence Force's security arrangements for the Sydney Olympic Games. The IRR provided a composite troop (designated 'D Troop') to the Australian contribution to the 2003 invasion of Iraq. This troop formed part of the Special Forces

ABOVE LEFT: Sapper Shaun Ward with an EDD locate a large drug plantation.

ABOVE RIGHT: Leading Aircraftwoman Vanessa Wallis, the first Australian female MWD handler to see active service.

BELOW: An Airfield Defence Guard patrol with No. 2 Airfield Defence Squadron (2AFDS) returns from a patrol after an arduous day searching for possible enemy threats to RAAF Base Tindal in Timor-Leste.

ABOVE: MPD handler Aaron Barnett on patrol in Timor-Leste.
BELOW: Wall of steel – soldiers with the International Stabilization
Force hold their position with Armoured Personal Carriers
and MWDs at the ready to contain an incident during a practice
response at a military range outside Dili, in Timor-Leste.

ABOVE: Australian United Nations peacekeepers on patrol in Timor-Leste to prevent border raids.

BELOW: EDD Kylie and Corporal James Hoy after a security search at Honiara International Airport, Solomon Islands. EDDs required constant access to water given the extremes of humidity in places like the Solomons.

ABOVE: A memorial for a group of very special fallen diggers – EDDs and their handlers killed in action while deployed on Operation Slipper – was unveiled in a corner of the Australian recreation area at Tarin Kowt, Oruzgan province, Afghanistan, in July 2011.

ABOVE: A MRTF 1 Engineer and his EDD take up a cordon position during a search for Taliban weapons caches during Operation Shak Haliwel. The dogs are very effective and are hated by the Taliban.

BELOW: EDD Bundy inside a Bushmaster armoured vehicle on patrol in the Mirabad Valley, with his handler Sapper David Brown, Afghanistan.

ABOVE LEFT: Aircraftman Ian Moore of 321 Expeditionary Combat Support Squadron, maintains a strong hold on Abra, while on night patrol during Exercise Pitch Black in 2008.

ABOVE RIGHT: Corporal John Cannon and EDD Storm from 1 CER Darwin search for weapons and explosives caches during a reconstruction mission in southern Afghanistan.

BELOW: EDD Harry rests in a moment of reflection before a picture of his pal Herbie and Herbie's handler Sapper Darren Smith, who were killed in action together.

ABOVE: The thin blue line, the sharp end of a RAAF military working dog protecting RAAF assets.

BELOW: Sapper Reuben Griggs snacks on some chocolate with EDD Que watching on at a patrol base in Afghanistan.

Task Group and is reported to have operated with the Australian Special Air Service Regiment within Iraq. IRR personnel have also formed part of subsequent Special Forces deployments, including the current deployment to Afghanistan. As part of this deployment IRR have EDD teams attached from Combat Engineers to work alongside Special Force members. These handlers, however, do not hand over their dogs but are a component part of the SF team in-situ.

Special Forces have had an on-off relationship with MWDs. They have been among the pioneers in their use as patrol/scout dogs, with teams parachuting well behind enemy lines to help detect German patrols in WWII. The British Parachute Regiment has had a long association with military dogs. Para dogs jumped during the European invasion and at Arnhem. Special Forces units around the world agree that the only real concern they have when on infiltration missions behind enemy lines is with enemy dogs. So convinced are Special Forces of the value of dogs, they are incorporating them into their own missions to aid detect explosives and enemy forces. Such units as Delta Force, British and Australian SAS regiments and Spetnaz all have MWD teams in their arsenals.

Modern technology has not eliminated the operational prospective for the military employment of dogs to support Special Operations Forces (SOF). Canine olfactory superiority, advanced hearing and the ability to detect movement offer significant military employment potential. Dogs can be trained for scouting, patrolling, building and ship searches, counter-mine, counter-drug and tracking to name a few roles. When used properly, they are an inexpensive and efficient force multiplier.

Nearly every SOF mission can benefit from the inclusion of dogs, particularly in stability and support operations conducted in developing countries which cannot employ or sustain complex and technologically sophisticated equipment. Military working dogs are a proven, low-technology, combat and combat-support capability and will have a future role in support of Special Operations Forces.

Special Forces units often use the night-time environment as a force multiplier when attacking superior numbers and forces without sophisticated night-surveillance equipment. With MWDs, SF are finding another weapons system they can utilise to their advantage. Australian SF MWDs are used to indicate the presence of ambush or the presence of enemy forces in Afghanistan.

In Australia there are several SF teams within the ADF (I am not specifically naming any here). An example of how they could be used is in the attack role in anti-terrorist operations. Belgian and German Shepherds seem to be the preferred breeds. SF dogs tend to be used in a four-person team, which consists of two dog handlers and two other troopers. A suspected building may be assaulted by explosive entry via door or by throwing the MWD through a window. The MWD acts as both a distraction and attack element in its own right. They are ideal in a situation where hostages are involved because they are a less than lethal force option. If the terrorist is attacked, all well and good; if a hostage is accidently bitten, then no serious harm has occurred to the operation. Likewise MWD can be thrown out of a semi-moving vehicle to both attack and distract the enemy while the SF vehicle comes to a halt and troops deploy.

Our Special Operations Task Group, Afghan National Security Forces and Coalition Forces have conducted counter-insurgency operations in the northern Oruzgan province of Afghanistan. During these operations insurgent weapons, munitions and improvised explosive device components were recovered. On several similar such missions EDDs operated by Special Forces soldiers were used.

Interestingly, in 2011 the US Special Forces were seen in the media to use a MWD as part of SEAL Team 6 which raided the residence of Bin Laden. This dog was most likely dual-trained in attack and explosive detection work. It was claimed that the dog was suited out in a bullet-proof vest and had a micro camera and handler-to-canine communications system attached. The elite Israeli defence forces canine unit, OKETZ, also uses this system and it is regarded as high-tech equipment. In Australia in 1972 an Engineer officer called George Hulse was testing the concept of canine recon using dogs at night via remote communication control. At the time this technology consisted of a dog-mounted radio, the TT626CA (then a very secret piece of kit), a canine ear piece for receiving commands, a micro switch that activated when the dog sat for more than ten seconds, plus a beacon for locating the dog. A micro camera was also produced for the dog, all this some 41 years prior to its use on the battlefield today.

9.

ARMY ENGINEERS

Military Working Dogs save lives. Plain and simple. In Afghanistan and Iraq, they are at the point of the bayonet. They step into the dark and unknown for the safety and well being of others and are the decisive difference.

John Carey
Lieutenant Colonel
CO 2 CER

Long before the recent upsurge in terrorism throughout the world, military units have relied on dogs for their innate scenting abilities. Though sentry duty, long-range tracking and man-trailing are probably the best known uses for military canines throughout history, it also stands to reason that these forces would also have the most pressing need for a safe and accurate method of detecting deadly explosives, a fact of life in the military environment. Enter the Explosive Detection Dog or EDD.

The Army Engineers did operate a Mine Detection Dog program as far back as 1952, when Australians operated British-trained MDDs during the Korean War. Though the Australian

Army Mine Dog program has since been discontinued, the links to the British Army, through training and operational methodology, continue to the present day. The British Army's vast experience with the detection of explosives and weapons, learned from over 30 years of constant operations in Northern Ireland, continues to be passed on to the Royal Australian Engineers. Today EDDs are used in a specialist search capacity within the Reconstruction Task Force to counter the threat of improvised explosive devices throughout Oruzgan province in Afghanistan. The EDD's tasks include the safe and accurate detecting of firearms and explosives. And, due to a mine's explosive contents, EDDs can still locate mines.

In 1953 the School of Military Engineering (SME) in Sydney began training dogs for both guard and mine detection. As in several other Commonwealth countries, the Australian dogs were trained using British Army doctrine. With the passage of time, the Infantry took over the tracker dogs and the RAAF took over the training of guard dogs. The call for mine dogs diminished with the termination of the Malayan Emergency Mine Dogs section at SME in 1959.

In 1971 the Army decided to re-introduce mine and explosive detecting dogs in response to a growing combat casuality list caused through mines and improvised explosive devices in the Vietnam War. Australian involvement in that war ceased in 1972.

Australia's participation in the war in South Vietnam was notorious for the number of casualties suffered from landmines, placed in what is technically termed a 'nuisance minefield'. Nuisance mining differs from 'planned mining' in that the nuisance minefield can contain one mine, or hundreds of them. It can be a mixture of manufactured mines and locally made improvised explosive devices (IED). Or it can be just one IED on its own.

It can be positioned in a village, on the side of a road, along a track or anywhere in the jungle. The nuisance miner pays no heed to the requirements of the Geneva Convention, which stipulates that planned minefields be fenced and signs warning of the presence of mines be erected in full view of anyone approaching it. Many countries have signed an international treaty agreeing never to use landmines in warfare again.

In addition, there were booby traps which were either IEDs or manufactured explosive devices such as hand grenades, rigged to explode when an unwary person activated it by picking up or moving something to which it was attached. Sometimes children were the unwitting victims of a booby trap concealed in a cold box (like an Esky) full of soft drinks – a grenade would be attached to a can of soft drink and would explode when the can was picked up. Generally the booby-trapped soft drink can was several cans down in the box so that a number of soldiers might gather around the child, buying soft drinks, and then, when the deadly can was reached, the explosion would kill or maim the carrier and others near the blast.

Not all booby traps or mines were activated by a person standing or moving them. Many were activated by a trip wire attached to the device; sometimes it was a taut wire across a track, designed to be activated on the slightest touch by a human. These were called 'tight' trip wires and could often be triggered by the wind, moving tree branches, birds and animals. Alternatively, 'loose' trip wires could tolerate some movement without triggering their explosive charge. These were often positioned to the sides of a track or road in order to trap soldiers moving off the line of advance when a fire fight between the soldiers and the enemy began. Australian soldiers preferred, at times, to patrol off to the sides of a track or road and these devices were employed to account for that manoeuvre. Occasionally, a trip wire activated a non-explosive device such as a swinging mace or high-energy animal trap which would cause serious injury without the use of explosives.

But it was the use of manufactured and improvised explosives which caused the worst injuries. These inflicted serious penetrating wounds, amputations, blindness, deafness and, very often, death. They were a weapon of fear.

In the Australian-controlled province of Phuoc Tuy, there was no shortage of explosives for the Viet Cong and North Vietnamese Army to access and use. They were supplied with Chinese (Chicom) explosives, generally TNT blocks, captured explosives of US origin such as TNT and C4 plastic explosive, unexploded bombs and artillery/mortar ammunition and an unending supply of the M16A1 bounding mine or M16 (not to be confused with the M16 rifle). This unending supply of M16 mines came from a huge Australian-laid minefield stretching almost 10 kilometres, from the 'Horseshoe' feature to the northwest of the Long Hai Hills, right along and parallel to these hills, and finishing near the seaside village of Lang Phuoc Hai. The minefield was a tactical blunder by the Australians, a story too complicated to be recounted here. Suffice to say that the enemy raided this minefield on numerous occasions and removed a high number of M16 mines, which were then employed in a nuisance minefield role, throughout the length and breadth of the Australian-controlled province.

The M16 mine was of US origin and was used by Australian troops as well until Australia became a signatory to the UN Mine Ban Treaty. It was a deadly device. Unlike other weapons, most of which require someone to point and shoot, mines are triggered by the 'victims', in that they are designed to explode when someone trips over or handles them. Landmines do not 'distinguish' between soldiers and civilians. They kill or maim a child playing football with the same ease as a soldier on patrol.

Mines were fitted with the silent M605 fuse mechanism – the victim would tread on it without realising he had done so (there was no audible 'click'). The fuse remains inert for a few seconds and then initiates the mine. The mine 'bounds' into the air – hence its description as a 'bounding mine' – and since the soldier who activated it has by now moved a few paces, the mine explodes between him and the man behind him, claiming both of them as its victims. One exploding M16 mine is known to have claimed seven Australian victims.

All combat soldiers had the responsibility to be aware of mines and IEDs. It was the job of the Australian Combat Engineer sapper, and at times the Infantry Assault Pioneer, to find and disarm any such device before it claimed a victim. It was a most difficult task requiring a high level of concentration by the sappers who were searching for them, and a high degree of personal control once one was detected and needed to be disarmed and removed from the ground. Unfortunately, many of the mine searches were activated when one went off after a soldier had stepped on it. Occasionally, our soldiers saw a mine in the ground in their immediate area, but generally speaking, this was a rare and lucky reprieve.

Something had to be done to find the mines and IED before our soldiers activated them. We used electronic devices such as the so-called 'mine detector', which detected metal not explosives, plus the use of mine 'prodders' – handheld probing devices, often bayonets. Prodders were used to remove camouflage from the mine and to feel the ground for soft spots where mines were buried, and then the subsequent hard touch where the prodder made contact with the mine casing. However, these processes were very time-consuming and were generally only employed when mines and IEDs were either seen, suspected or had been activated – where there was one mine, there was almost always another in the vicinity.

There had to be a better and more efficient method of finding mines and explosives. In 1969 the US Army decided to retro-research the use of mine-detecting dogs. Their Veterinary Corps had an established dog breeding program in Maryland under the control of Lieutenant Colonel Michael Castleberry. At the same time, it initiated its Bio-Sensor Research Laboratory at the Aberdeen Proving Ground, also in Maryland, under the control of a very savvy canine psychologist, John Romba.

Romba had a number of dogs that he trained and tested using a variety of methods. He tested the sensitivity of a dog's olfactory senses (smell) by training the dog to respond to infinitely tiny particles of explosive substances in a device he called 'The Olfactometer'. So successful were his training and testing techniques that he was contracted by the US Department of Defense to produce a training regime for Infantry off-leash dogs with the specific intent of service in South Vietnam searching for mines and tunnels. The training processes and procedures were designed at the United States Army Infantry School at Fort Benning in Georgia, and the first course was conducted at the end of 1970. Australian Army Headquarters sent Captain George Hulse, RAE, to attend the course and report on its potential for use by Australian troops in Vietnam. Hulse had commanded Australian combat engineers here and had a wealth of knowledge and experience in mine and tunnel warfare. He was very impressed by the efficiency of the dog teams in finding mines, explosives, weapons caches, ammunition, trip wires and tunnels. He recommended the immediate establishment of an Australian Army explosive dog training and research wing. Australian Army HQ reacted immediately and raised the Mine Dog Wing at the School of Military Engineering at Moorebank in NSW, with Hulse as the officer commanding and research officer.

Hulse recruited 20 personnel, many of whom were National Servicemen, and acquired 16 dogs of varying breeds. Some dogs were donated, some were bought from the public, and one dog was recruited as a stray when it was seen running around near the SME front gate. The dog kennels were built by the sappers at SME. The training was intensive and there was a sense of urgency in every session conducted. The reason for this was clear. This group of sappers and their dogs was going to Vietnam to detect mines and explosives in areas where these devices had caused much pain and suffering to our troops. Every session was noted on a form designed to record the performance of every dog team, during every training session. The dogs were trained in passive search techniques, which means that the dog did not become excited and want to play with the detected device. The dog was required to adopt the 'sit' position about 60 centimetres from and facing the device it detected.

Army HQ needed assurance that the Australian EDDs would be operationally fit for service prior to their deployment to Vietnam. A trial was designed to test the efficiency of the dog teams. It occurred at the Tropical Trials Establishment at Tully in far north Queensland where a large number of mines, booby traps, explosives and trip wires were positioned in a variety of nuisance mine situations, similar to those experienced in Vietnam. The trial was designed by a Defence Department scientist, Dr Oliver Raymond, whose job was to report on the performance of the

RAE dog teams. He was assisted by observers from other Corps, particularly the Royal Australian Infantry. Dr Raymond had laid the mines up to three months prior to the arrival of the dog teams for the trial. Some of the mines were underwater. The trial was a success, albeit there were understandable 'misses' by some of the dog teams. However, the mines which were underwater were detected, much to the amazement of all involved in the trial.

In early 1972, the Military Dog Wing went on notice for service in Vietnam. Volunteer dog handlers stepped forward and 12 of the most efficient explosive detecting dogs were selected to serve, under the command of Hulse, as a part of the 1st Field Squadron Group RAE at Nui Dat. At the time when the group was undertaking pre-embarkation administrative procedures, the prime minister of Australia, William McMahon, announced that Australia would commence a withdrawal of all combat troops from the Vietnam War, beginning in mid-1972. This announcement caused the cancellation of the Engineer dog teams to Vietnam.

In the 1970s, and not for the first or last time, Army dog teams supported the Australian Federal Police and NSW Police Force on anti-drug and explosive detection operations. Engineer dog teams were deployed to search aircraft at Sydney International Airport when a bomber made a threat to destroy a passenger jet. Two dog teams were rushed by police escort to the airport, the plane was searched and declared clear of explosives, and it was permitted to return to service immediately. Another incident occurred as a result of a bomber firing an explosive charge in front of the Yugoslav Travel Agency adjacent to the Capitol Theatre in the Haymarket in Sydney. No one was injured in the blast, but it was a taste of terrorism in Sydney.

The Saturday night following the blast, the same bomber phoned the NSW Police and claimed that he had placed a bomb in the Capitol Theatre, and that the bomb would go off at 8 PM when the theatre was full for the show *Jesus Christ Superstar*. This time,the entire Mine Dog Wing from SME was activated and rushed by both Military Police and NSW Police escorts to the Capitol Theatre. The Engineer dog teams arrived at 7.15 PM and assisted in evacuating the people from the theatre through emergency exits. As the last person left the building, the search was handed over to Hulse and begun in earnest. The Capitol was searched from the roof to the basement. This included Sergeant 'Billy' Unmeopa scaling a rope dangling over the stage so that he could check the gantries holding the over-stage lights and special effects machinery.

At 7.55 PM, Hulse ordered the dog teams out of the building and together with Sergeant Unmeopa, Sapper Les Sheather and his dog Sabre, headed toward an exit via a back door. But then, high drama. On his way to the exit, Sabre suddenly pulled away from Sheather and ran to the rear of a decorative column situated against the interior wall of the theatre and sat very convincingly. He had found a tightly closed metal toolbox secreted behind the column. It was now 7.58 PM, two minutes to the threatened detonation time. After attaching a 'pulling hook' and long line to the box, Hulse, Unmeopa, Sheather and Sabre made a bolt for the exterior of the building. Informing the Police inspector of the find, the sappers put fingers in ears and then pulled on the pulling hook. There was a loud crash as the toolbox was yanked free of the column and then the sounds of metal pieces hitting a concrete floor. But there was no explosion. So Hulse, Unmeopa, Sheather and Sabre waited for a few minutes before venturing back into the theatre again. They found an explosive-powered nailing gun, with a number of charges scattered around it. There was no bomb, but they were delighted with Sabre's 'find'. *Jesus*

Christ Superstar was restartedand the audience enjoyed the rest of their evening. There were many police callouts during 1972, and both the AFP and NSW Police were convinced of the benefit of dog teams in assisting them with their operations.

In 1972 the Australian Customs Service attached one of their preventive officers, David Raynor, to the second explosive detecting dog course at the SME and he graduated as a proficient EDD handler. By the end of that year, the Engineer Mine Dog Wing had attended a number of exercises in Australian military training areas, supporting infantry and armoured units. This experience demonstrated the value of engineer dog teams attached to combat units. An attempt was made to parachute dogs when Hulse attended a parachute refresher course at RAAF Base Williamstown. However, as happened on a previous occasion, the RSPCA advised against it, based on concerns about risks to the health of the dog, and so no canine parachuting of Australian Army dogs was undertaken at that time.

The Mine Dog Wing was renamed the Explosive Detecting Dog Wing in the early 1980s due to an increased focus on countering urban terrorism. Because Australia was a signatory to the UN Mine Ban Treaty, the word 'mine' was thought to be inappropriate. The wing has remained at SME as an explosive detection dog-training base to this day.

Like their peers all over the world in peacetime, many of the dog handlers' efforts seem to go unnoticed. Many handlers have spent careers establishing the ADF's canine capabilities between the well-advertised operations such as Vietnam and Somalia, East Timor and Afghanistan. It is in the gaps, sometimes 20 years long, that handlers have kept the trade alive. It is to these peacetime ADF Doggies that we owe much.

Many commanders do not even know MWDs are part of

their assets. One such experience happened to Shaun 'Bluey' Forde, who was Chief Dog Trainer and spent many years at SME advancing the use of EDDs only to find, when the Engineers finally had an overseas operation, that the CO did not deploy dogs because he did not know he had any. Shaun served in the ADF from 1977 to 1989 and was involved in multiple peace-time operations, including embassy searches, World Expo and the Commonwealth Games.

MWDs serve in all three Combat Engineer Regiments (CER). The 1st Combat Engineer Regiment (1 CER), based in the Northern Territory and attached to 1st Brigade, is a Regular Army unit of the Royal Australian Engineers and is tasked with providing mobility and counter-mobility support.

The 2nd Combat Engineer Regiment (2 CER) traces its history back to the 4th Field Company, Royal Australian Engineers, which was renamed the 7th Field Company on 20 September 1915. As of 2011, 2 CER was the largest combat engineer unit in the Australian Army. Throughout its history, individual members of the unit have been involved in operations in Cambodia, Somalia, Pakistan, Rwanda, Solomon Islands and Bougainville, and giving support to police during several Commonwealth Heads of Government Meetings (CHOGM). In addition to its military role, the regiment also works closely with the local Queensland community in times of emergency, such as during the 2011 floods.

A brief history of the 7th Field Company: it served with distinction in Egypt and France during WWI, where it saw action in the Battle of the Somme, Menin Road and the Hindenburg Line, before returning to Australia and disbanding on 23 May 1919.

In 1921 the unit was re-raised as the 7th Field Company of

the 1st Division, a militia (reserve). In 1941, the unit was called out for full-time service and gained 2nd Australian Imperial Force status during WWII. It served in New Guinea and fought against the Japanese at the Kokoda Track and Bougainville until the end of the war. When it returned to Australia, it was disbanded once again in 1946. Raised again in 1947, it was involved in several post-WWII operations and the Korean, Malayan Emergency and Indonesian conflicts. Over the 1970s and 1980s the Engineers were reorganised under many guises and name designations. In 1989 the UN, acting under Resolution 435, formed the United Nations Transitional Assistance Group (UNTAG) for deployment to the war-torn country of Namibia. The mission was to supervise the withdrawal of the South African Defence Force, assist those displaced by the war and pave the way for the first 'free and fair' elections ever held in that country.

Following the Force Structure Review in 1991, the 2nd/3rd Field Engineer Regiment was reformed into the 1st, 2nd and 3rd Combat Engineer Regiments. The 2nd Combat Engineer Regiment was raised first, on 24 November 1991, and remained at Enoggera. The oldest of the combat engineer regiments, 2 CER underwent a change during 1999 when it was assigned the task of forming and commanding the new Joint Incident Response Unit (JIRU) in support of the Sydney 2000 Olympic Games. The unit was split, with the majority of personnel moving to Holsworthy to form the JIRU and subsequently the new Incident Response Regiment (IRR), leaving a small Headquarters element and 7th Combat Engineer Squadron in Enoggera. In July 2001, the regiment underwent a force structure review which saw the unit grow in strength once again.

In 2001, a composite engineer troop was deployed to support the 4 RAR Battalion Group in East Timor and undertook a wide variety of construction and combat engineering tasks along the border between East and West Timor, returning again over 2003–04, (AUSBATT IX) and again in 2010. The 2nd Combat Engineer Regiment led the Reconstruction Task Force 2 (RTF 2), which deployed to Afghanistan from 2007 as part of Operation Slipper. The regiment's personnel were deployed in a wide variety of roles, including training and mentoring members of the Afghan National Army, and undertaking route clearance, search, construction tasks and infantry missions in an extremely high-risk environment. During 2010 2 CER deployed Engineer Task Unit 1 (ETU1) based on 24th Support Squadron and 7th Combat Engineer Squadron as part of the 750-strong 6 RAR Battle Group Mentoring Task Force (MTF1) group deployed to Oruzgan province. This was a very intense, dangerous and demanding deployment: two sappers and one EDD were killed in action and over 25 sappers wounded in action. During this period approximately 250 caches were discovered and approximately 180 IEDs identified. The regiment is expected to return to Afghanistan with MTF4 in 2012.

3rd Combat Engineer Regiment

The 1990 ADF Structure Review included a reorganisation of the divisional engineer structure and recommended the introduction of combat engineer regiments under the command of each brigade. Consequently, the 3rd Combat Engineer Regiment was raised in Townsville on 1 July 1992, the RAE Corps; birthday. In early 1993, the 17th Field Troop of the 18th Field Squadron served in Somalia as part of the 1st Battalion Group, Royal Australian Regiment (RAR) within a multinational force. Three EDDs were deployed, the first Army dogs on operations since Vietnam. In late 1994 and 1995 a section from the 18th Field

Squadron served in Rwanda as part of the United Nations Force to provide humanitarian assistance. In 1994 a detachment from the regiment deployed to Bougainville to assist in facilitating peace negotiations, and as a consequence of these, many members of the regiment served there with the Peace Monitoring Group between 1998 and 2003. In 1998 members of the regiment deployed to northern Papua New Guinea to provide emergency relief assistance to the victims of a tsunami. In 1998 an additional field squadron, the 16th Field Squadron, was raised in order to provide a field squadron to support each of the 1st and 2nd battalions, RAR.

From September 1999 to January 2000 the regiment served as part of the International Force East Timor. Subsequently, and under the auspices of the United Nations, squadrons have undertaken six-month tours of service in Timor.

In the first half of 2003 the 25th Support Squadron undertook the 62nd rotation of duties at Butterworth in Malaysia and a three-man EOD team served in Baghdad in the aftermath of the US invasion of Iraq. In the second half of 2003, the 18th Combat Engineer Squadron deployed as part of the Joint Interagency Task Force to restore law and order in the Solomon Islands.

In September 2005 personnel from the 25th Support Squadron deployed with very short notice on Operation Slipper to Afghanistan in support of the Special Forces Task Group. The engineer element assisted in the construction of the base camp and developing force protection. The regiment continued to support the task group with small detachments until it was withdrawn in September 2006.

From February to March 2006, 16 CE Sqn and the EDD section deployed on Operation Acolyte to Melbourne for the provision of a high-risk engineer search capability for the security of the Commonwealth Games. The regiment began preparations for deployment to Reconstruction Task Force 3 (RTF 3) in Afghanistan in 2008 and for a troop contribution to Operation Astute continuing the engineer presence in Timor-Leste (the name East Timor was changed to upon liberation).

All combat engineer regiments have taken turn to rotate through active service in Afghanistan. During the Reconstruction Task Force phase it was: firstly 1 CER, then 2 CER and 3 CER in 2007 and 2008. The fourth cycle was by 2 CER in 2008.

The Mentoring and Reconstruction Task Forces was initiated by 1 CER, followed by a 3 CER deployment. Then, during the Mentoring Task Force phase beginning in 2010, 2 CER initially commenced, followed by 1 CER in mid-2010 to mid-2011 period and continued with 3 CER in the second half of 2011.

SOMALIA

By late 1992, the catastrophic situation in Somalia had outstripped the UN's ability to quickly restore peace and stability, mainly because the UN was hamstrung by insufficient forces and its peacekeeping principles and methods could not cope with the need to use force in such complex situations. On 3 December 1992, UN Security Council Resolution 794 authorised a coalition of UN members led by the US to form the Unified Task Force (UNITAF) and intervene to protect the delivery of humanitarian assistance and restore peace. Australia sent three EDD teams from 3 CER Lavarack Barracks Townsville to operations in Somalia from January to May 1993. The dog handlers and EDDs sent to Somalia in 1993 were Seamus Doherty (EDD Mick), Simon Harvey (EDD Duke) and Darren Davis (EDD Tia).

The main base for the dog teams in Somalia was Baidoa Airfield where they lived with EOD and Ammunition Techs. There were initially five American Marine Corps EOD Techs but they eventually moved on to Mogadishu. The EDD teams' main role was search operations in Baidoa and Buurhakaba regions searching for weapon and ordnance caches. Vehicle check point duties were also included. However, most of their time was spent with Infantry sections patrolling and searching where necessary. The dogs were attached to 2 Platoon, A Company, 1st Battalion, the Royal Australian Regiment (RAR) as part of the Australian contingent to the UNITAF in Somalia. This battalion group was very successful at fostering and protecting humanitarian relief efforts and won widespread international praise for its efforts in restoring law and order and re-establishing functional legal, social and economic systems. Many Muslims fear dogs and so they proved a great force multiplier. All three dogs sent to Somalia returned to Australia under closely supervised quarantine regulations.

Once the dogs acclimatised they worked very well. The heat did affect them and they lost a large amount of weight because their diets had changed dramatically. Army supply stuffed up by not bringing enough dog food – the dogs ate MRE (meal, ready-to-eat) rations the same as the handlers, until more dog food was sent from Australia. Apart from that the dogs were well looked after thanks to the handlers. US Army Vet Captain Steve Waters was based in Mogadishu but came out to Baidoa to see the dogs regularly and the Engineers visited him with the dogs when they went to Mogadishu. He was based at the large US Embassy in Mogadishu. A focus point for many coalition forces, the US Embassy also contained the main military hospital in its grounds where daily intelligence briefings for the task group were held.

These dogs were the first service dogs to be allowed back into Australia. Prior to deployment the handlers were told that they would be either destroyed in Somalia or given to the embassy. The handlers protested. When the media got wind of it and the public spoke up, the dogs were put into quarantine for nine months – seven months in the UK and the remaining time in Sydney. It was cheaper to do this than to train another three dogs.

Of the dogs sent to Somalia, eventually Mick was teamed up with his handler Seamus after quarantine. Duke was retired and Tia was given to another handler. Mick and Tia were also deployed to Bougainville with new handlers (Seamus and Darrin had discharged from the Army at that time).

The Australian Army have employed working dogs since WWI in many roles and in different corps. The Royal Australian Engineer Corps explosive detection dogs have had a varied role supporting operations in the environments listed below:

EDD Operational Employment

1988	Expo 88, Brisbane
1993	Operation Solace, Somalia
1994	Operation Lagoon, Bougainville, Papua New Guinea
1997	US presidential visit, Port Douglas
1999	Operation Stabilise (VCPs – Weapon Cache Hides), East Timor
2000	Operation Gold, Sydney Olympics
2002	Commonwealth Heads of Government Meeting
2003	Operations Anode, Solomon Islands Weapons and Explosives
2003	Operation Scrummage, Rugby World Cup

2006	Operations Accolyte,
	Commonwealth Games, Melbourne
2006	Operation Astute, East Timor
2005	Operation Slipper, Afghanistan
	(weapons and IEDs)

To become an EDD handler in the Australian Army you must first become a combat engineer in the Royal Australian Engineers. From here you must apply for the EDD specialist course. Until recently the Army only employed male handlers in this role because it is classified a 'combat role', from which female personnel were exempted. However, in 2011 the first female EDD handler commenced the course at SME.

The first EDDs trained in the Australian Army were trained using British Army Veterinary Corp doctrine of the time, for an active response to the target. Warrant Officer Mick Peter Alyward, the Chief Dog Trainer of the RAVC in 1981, advised Captain Andy Francis Marks, the OC of the Australian Engineers Dogs, while Marks was in the UK on Longlook exchange between Australian and British forces. Marks was so impressed with the RAVC standard that Alyward was invited out to Australia the following year. Alyward culled many dogs and reintroduced the active response, which had lapsed at that time. Alyward saw much promise in Corporal Smiley Matthews at SME and helped arranged a Longlook attachment for him. Matthews undertook the RAVCs Guard Dog course, took dogs for operational use in Germany after he trained them and went on to training specialist dogs until his return from the six-month attachment.

At the time this type of target indication doctrine was considered acceptable, but since 1997 it has been phased out in favour of a passive response technique. Target indication teaches the dog to dig or initially retrieve the training aid, which can lead to a possible dangerous accident when dealing with explosives. Today, every Australian Army EDD is a passive-response, retrieve-reward, off-lead detection dog. The dog is trained to work the 'scent cone' from the "target odour' to the 'source'. Once the source is pinpointed, the dog offers conditioned passive response consisting of a 'sit' or 'down' position combined with an intensely focused stare at the source of the target odour. As can be imagined, in practice this method provides a very safe and accurate way of indicating the exact location of the source of the target odour, not just a generalised indication that the target odour exists in the area. The EDD is not taught to play with the source or target odour, or to expect a reward from the handler. Rather, the EDD is taught that the reward, generally a tennis ball, will always come from the exact point of the source, not from the handler or anywhere else. Trainers employ several ingenious methods of remotely delivering the reward to the dog. In the initial imprinting stages where the training environments can be more precisely controlled, this delivery is often via a tube located behind the source or projected from a radio-controlled delivery system. Later, during field work or further on during continuation training, the handler or an assistant is able to deliver the reward effectively by bouncing it next to the source. All EDDs are trained to detect explosives and propellants from all explosive sub-groups or families manufactured worldwide.

Conditioning the dog via these reward delivery methods develops the intense and accurate stare required to enable the EDD handler to direct a bomb technician to the exact location of the device from a safe distance. EDDs are trained to respond to both voice and hand signals. They can be directed from vast distances (100 metres plus) by the handler, who also has the ability, for example, to call the dog in, tell it to stop, go left, go right or go out further.

Solomon Islands

In 2003 the operation that utilised EDDs was Operation Anode, the regional assistance mission to the Solomon Islands. Over a year, 12 EDD teams rotated in and out of the country to support the Australian Federal Police on search operations.

The primary task of the EDDs on that operation was the detection and location of small arms weapons and ammunition believed to be stolen from Police armouries and in the hands of criminals.

EDDs were employed to conduct targeted operations on the premises of alleged criminals throughout the country, prevent weapons smuggling by searching air freight or passenger baggage and search ferries either at dock or at sea.

The dogs had a number of finds while in country and, probably more importantly, provided a massive psychological impact on the local population after demonstrations of their capabilities were given across the country. Many weapons were turned over to the Police purely out of fear of the dogs and their ability to find caches.

East Timor

EDDs teams were deployed to East Timor as part of Operation Warden. The teams were used in a variety of pro-active and reactive search operations with the RAE search teams and Royal Australian infantry vehicle check points.

Today, the Army EDD teams' primary role is deployment overseas on ADF operations. In the event of enactment of the Defence Aid to Civil Community (DACC) federal legislation, EDD teams can be used in the public sector. In the past this has included assistance at the 2000 Olympics, 2002 Commonwealth Heads of Government Meeting (CHOGM) and the 2003 Rugby World Cup.

Defence, as part of the overall Australian Government contribution, worked alongside the Victoria Police to provide security for the Commonwealth Games, called Operation Acolyte. Acolyte is Latin for helper or assistant and was chosen to symbolise the Defence supporting role in the staging of the Commonwealth Games. Operation Acolyte included approximately 2600 ADF personnel, from across the three services, performing a range of specialist roles to provide security, ceremonial and general support. These extra troops were accommodated at, and working from, existing Defence establishments in and around Melbourne, including Simpson Barracks, Watsonia; Maygar Barracks, Broadmeadows; RAAF Williams, Laverton and Point Cook, and Victoria Barracks, Melbourne. Part of the security measures was support from the Army's EDD teams that conducted both preventive searches and emergency standby for any terrorist bomb threat.

Some other recent operations using dog teams were Operation Anode to the Solomon Islands where 12 EDD teams rotated in country over a 12-month period in support of the AFP, and deployment to Somalia (as part of the UNITAF), East Timor, Bougainville and Afghanistan. The CERs are used extensively within Afghanistan in villages during search operations for arms hides as well as the detection of IEDs and also for vehicle checkpoint work.

Australia has deployed ADF Reconstruction Task Forces (RTF), consisting of a combined arms team, to the Oruzgan province in southern Afghanistan as part of Operation Slipper. The RTF was in partnership with the Netherlands Provincial Reconstruction Team (PRT) and formed part of the NATO-led International Security Assistance Force. The Netherlands are no longer involved with this project. The RTF had a clearly defined role to work on reconstruction, improvement of provincial infrastructure and community-based projects. The RTF also provided trade training to the local population and military engineering training to the Afghan National Army. This type of assistance is designed to benefit the people of Oruzgan province well into the future and hopefully form building blocks of a future stable and prosperous community. The RTF contained around 370 ADF personnel from predominately Queensland-based units. It included elements to provide command, security, engineering, and administrative support and was equipped with Bushmaster Infantry Mobility Vehicles (IMV), Australian Light Armoured Vehicles (ASLAVs) and armoured engineer plant equipment. Australia's contribution to ISAF was an important component of the Australian government's commitment to assist Afghanistan achieve a stable and secure future. The Task Force's initial role and name changed to the Mentoring and Reconstruction Task Force (MRTF) and now to Mentoring Task Force (MTF).

Defence spokesperson Brigadier Nikolic said that

the actions of the Explosive Detection Dogs had saved lives. Improvised devices placed on public roads are designed to kill and maim people. Explosive Detection Dogs are used by the task force in a specialist search capacity to counter the high threat of improvised explosive devices throughout Oruzgan province. The task force maintains an Explosive Detection Dog capability providing the required level of force protection for deployed Australian troops.

The Australian contribution to ISAF in Afghanistan has focused on the Special Forces fight against the Taliban within Oruzgan and North Helmand provinces. However, the 440-person MRTF has been very active in southern Afghanistan rebuilding structure and training the Army and Police forces. Within this group the Australian Engineers have deployed EDD teams. The aim of the counter-insurgency operations in Oruzgan was to disrupt the enemy and remove their capability to threaten both coalition forces and the local Afghan people.

A typical EDD working day report recorded:

The Explosive Detection Dogs are a key tool in locating insurgent improvised explosive devices (IEDs) and weapons caches. As the pair search, their fellow engineers work to rebuild a bridge on Afghanistan's Highway 1, which had been destroyed by insurgent explosives. The four-day operation was concentrated on conducting cordons and searches of local compounds (Qualas). These searches yielded several caches of explosives and ammunition. These caches were searched and their contents destroyed in an explosion controlled by Australian Engineers.

Today's Army EDDs provide support to the ADF and civilian government agencies in the detection of improvised explosive devices, explosives, ammunition and weapons. MWDs have been used for centuries as messengers, combatants and for security, and more recently as mine and explosive detection dogs. EDDs are trained to locate their targets – bombs, weapons, explosives – and communicate this to their handlers. EDDs and their predecessors, the tracker dogs, have deployed overseas to Vietnam, Somalia, Bougainville, East Timor and to Afghanistan.

The EDD Section of 3 CER is based in Townsville, Queensland. The Dog section is a sub-unit of the Specialist Troop of 3 CER. The Specialist Troop contains many tradesmen such as carpenters and joiners, plumbers and pipefitters. In June 2009, the EDD Section had a posted strength of six EDD handlers, three of whom were on deployment in Afghanistan. The role of the section is to provide support in search tasks for 3 CER and also units of the 3rd Brigade. The 3 CER has a unit mascot in the kennels fostered by the EDD Section. His name is Wooley, a Dingo. Wooley is a traditional Army name for the Dingo as it comes from Woolston Barooma; however, a dingo back in 1986 was called Bruiser. Today's Wooley is the fourth to hold the title. As a member of the unit the mascot has traditionally had free rein around the camp, and is often seen sleeping in its handler's barracks. Unfortunately, from time to time, like all diggers he would get in trouble. On one occasion he bailed up some female soldiers, was demoted and restricted to barracks for several days.

EDD section enjoys some autonomy in its training role. It is commanded and administered by the Specialist Troop command and control element through a sergeant and lieutenant troop commander. All handlers and EDDs are trained at SME, after which the dog team is posted to a unit where continuation training further develops the skill sets for both handler and dog. The stimuli for the dogs includes all the inventory of service explosives available in the ADF plus black powder and other explosives used in quarry work. The explosives are stored in an explosives kit, which can only be accessed by the EDD staff so the possibility of contamination of odours and scents is minimised. The explosive kits are controlled by the unit Q Store. However, there is very tight control maintained on the issue of the day-to-day explosives used in continuation training by the EDD section commander and second in command.

Caption Robert Ellison recently returned from overseas operations and has made the following recommendations for the Management of Explosive Detection Dog Capability.

16 CE SQN and other attachments from 3 CER have recently returned to Australia following their deployment to Afghanistan as part of the Mentoring and Reconstruction Task Force (MRTF-2) on Op Slipper. Several of the issues experienced during the operation were not new or unique to MRTF-2 but were a recurring issue common to previous operations within the Middle East Area of Operations (MEAO). One such issue is the efficient management of the Explosive Detection Dog (EDD) capability within the MEAO.

Nearly all of the problems experienced when attempting to improve the management of the EDD capability are born from a lack of Explosive Detection Dog Handlers (EDDH) within the Army. Army does not have a large pool of EDDH to draw from to cater for the demands of current operations, although excellent efforts from SME in the last 18 months are starting to allay this problem. Additional pressures on manning requirements may include R&R relief, the requirements for EDDH personnel to conduct training, career courses, postings as an instructor to School of Military Engineering (SME) and for the conduct of leave and recuperation prior to the next operation. The restrictions that may be incurred from a reduced manning capacity emphasise the need for the most efficient management of the EDDH capability within the MEAO.

Ideally a balanced approach should manage the employment of this limited capability in such a way which enables the satisfaction of the operational need and still allows the capability to grow within the Corps (group need) and does not 'burn out' our EDDH and EDD (individual need).

Currently and in recent history, the dispositions of EDD teams within the MEAO consist of an EDD Section allocated to RTF/ MRTF/ MTF and a Section to Special Operations Task Group (SOTG). The EDD Section belonging to the MRTF usually consists of three teams usually drawn from the parent unit/brigade with shortfalls supplemented by external combat engineer units and School of Military Engineering (SME) as available. There is a similar FE dedicated to deploy in support of Special Operations Task Group. The parent unit for this FE is the IRR.

Ideally, there would be an Explosive Detection Dog team with every Combat Engineer Search Section. This would ensure better synchronisation of support to all manoeuvre elements through their dedicated search section, including the EDD team, and would also permit the team to employ a more reliable work/ rest cycle. This of course is not achievable either currently or in the foreseeable future. Due to the limited supply of the EDD search asset they cannot be dedicated to support a particular FE. They must instead be allocated according to the risks associated with each mission and according to the commander's priorities for support. This in turn drives the need for a single and central commander to plan, implement and manage the allocation of the EDD capability among all FE. This is traditionally conducted by the Royal Australian Engineer Combat Engineer Squadron Headquarters upon advice from the EDD Section Commander, due to the fact that the EDD Section Commander is usually outside the wire with his EDD in support of the manoeuvre element. To maximise the potential for the Section Commander to manage the EDD capability it would be preferable that he is separate to the three EDD teams and remains in Multinational Barracks Tarin Kowt (MNBTK) to command the Section. There are also many other duties that may be better managed by the presence of a dedicated EDD Section Commander based in MNBTK such as: the work, rest and training cycle of each EDD team including the requirement to return to MNBTK for one week in every three weeks to conduct buried hide training; the management of additional support requirements for the other-than-scheduled operational tasks within the area of operations including support to the commanding officers's countless logistic resupply moves and supporting special events such as the MNBTK market search; the maintenance and management of buried hides in Multinational Barracks Tarin Kowt ; the coordination of food resupply to the EDD; the provision of specialist advice to the Squadron Commander; the facilitation of a technical chain of command back to Australia for lessons learnt and changes in enemy standard operational procedures. the conduct of informal liaison with AQIS for the return of Explosive Detection Dog to Australia and the conduct of operations assessments and reteams for new explosive detection dog teams. The Explosive Detection Dog Section Commander could also deploy out of synch with each successive Brigade rotation. This would enable him to assist in the coordination of the intra-theatre movement and reception of the EDD teams in addition to the provision of initial training for EDD teams new to the theatre of operations.

Regardless of any short-term solution for future operations

in the MEAO, the effective management of a vital and very limited asset such as the EDD teams is likely to remain an issue of concern. As operations in the MEAO continue the number of Explosive Detection Dog Handlers arriving in theatre for their second and third tours are likely to increase. This may also have an adverse effect upon the retention of these members. The only solid and reliable long-term solution that will address the needs of the operation, the group and the individual is to train more Explosive Detection Dog and Explosive Detection Dog Handlers.

The Army Engineer Dog handlers receive a great deal of training in the art of general high-risk search, engineering and explosive identification prior to selection as an EDD handler. This ensures soldiers have the best possible training and preparation for their role as EDD handlers.

Sapper Stuart Conlin, Royal Australian Engineers

One example of the experience an engineer may have prior to becoming a handler is Sapper Stuart Conlin, Royal Australian Engineers.

In October 2003, Stuart joined the Australian Army and attended his recruit training at Kapooka in New South Wales. In December he graduated from recruit training and was allotted to the RAE. He marched into the SME based at Steele Barracks at Moorebank, near Liverpool, New South Wales, and attended his Initial Employment Training course as a field engineer.

On graduation, Stuart was posted to 9 Field Squadron of 1 CER based at Robertson Barracks in Darwin. Stuart was sent to Banda Aceh after the tsunami hit that Indonesian city in January

2005 and returned to Darwin in March. As a combat engineer, Stuart attended several engineer courses in preparation for deployment to Afghanistan, which occurred in September 2006.

Afghanistan: First Deployment

Stuart operated as a combat engineer using mine equipment to check roads and other routes for explosive devices. The patrols outside their base were at Tarin Kowt with Reconstruction Task Force 1 (RTF 1). One of the main tasks was to prepare the base and secure the area for RTF 2. Tarin Kowt received excessive rocket attacks from the enemy during this period. The Taliban were more intent on fire and movement at that time, and Stuart's group did not have the same threat of improvised explosive devices as he was to experience on future deployment to Afghanistan.

During this deployment, Stuart became interested in the work being undertaken by the engineer dog teams. He demonstrated a talent for dog work to the engineer dog team who were present at that time – Corporal Damian Dunne, Lance Corporal Alistair Leviere and Sapper Adam Exalby. They gave Stuart some on-the-job training and he took to the work with zeal. On his return to Australia, Stuart returned to 1 CER at Robertson Barracks in Darwin.

Detection Dog Training

Corporal John Cannon arrived at the dog section of 1 CER in late 2007 and Stuart received training from John until being allocated an EDD handlers course at SME in February 2008. The course ran for 15 months and Stuart was teamed up with EDD Solo, a cross Labrador.

Solo was originally found wandering the streets of Liverpool one morning by Sapper Zeke Smith who was driving to SME.

Zeke had to save Solo from being hit by a car. He called the dog over, put him in the car and took him to the dog kennels at SME. The officer commanding the kennels agreed to look after Solo until his owner could be located and the dog returned. Despite searches and notifications, no-one claimed the dog.

At the completion of the EDD course, Stuart and Solo were posted to 3 CER based at Lavarack Barracks in Townsville. Much of 2008 was spent ramping up for operational duty in Afghanistan and in October Stuart and Solo passed their operational assessment for overseas deployment.

Afghanistan: Second Deployment
Stuart and Solo were deployed to Mentoring RTF 2 (MRTF 2) in Afghanistan on 26 May 2009. They flew by civil air charter from Townsville to Darwin and then on to Kuwait. From Kuwait to Tarin Kowt was by C130 (Hercules) military transport aircraft. Stuart and Solo were a part of the advance party and on arrival at Tarin Kowt they were given in-country and medical training for about three days. Acclimatisation in the dry 55-degree Celsius heat was a problem for a short time. Stuart met up again with Corporal John Cannon and Sapper Brett Turley, who were in the process of leaving Afghanistan at the completion of their rotation. Stuart continued his preparation for deployment into the field. This took about two weeks when the dogs were introduced to the Afghanistan explosives and other scent pictures being experienced on operations.

Solo was to find his first improvised explosive device (IED) on Operation 'Rebel I'. The IED was three mortar bombs linked to a Russian anti-personnel mine. In Stuart's words:

I sent Solo into a search to check out a position near Patrol Base

'Overwatch' where friendly troops form up where they can watch a road or sector of ground, particularly where our vehicles might travel through. Solo found the IED buried in an old fire pit. I believe that the intention of the enemy was to fire at us from the Green Zone, causing us to dive for cover in any hole in the ground and that would have been enough to set off this IED. Solo was pleased with himself and I was delighted with Solo, he got to play with his tennis ball, and I sat around the overwatch position for the rest of the day with a big grin on my face. Our infantry mates were really happy with Solo and that did a lot to build up their trust in the EDD team.

But it was not all easy going. Stuart and Solo were to become the victims of an IED themselves. Stuart:

We were at a Support Base one morning where the ground was rock hard. I heard no disturbances and things looked quite normal. I sent Solo up the centre of the road and we were followed by a couple of combat engineers. A Bushmaster was following about 25 metres behind us when I heard an enormous bang and the force of it knocked me over. I was not wounded but the shock of the explosion was unsettling. Solo was a bit apprehensive about things and about 30 minutes later we continued to search. Solo continued to need concentrated dog handling to keep him interested in his job for about three days. After that, he continued to work well but was very conscious of loud bangs. Rifle fire did not bother him, just very loud explosions. This IED went off about 200 meteres away from where another IED had exploded before and that one involved my mate Sapper Reuben Griggs and his EDD Nova. The after-IED investigation concluded that the IED had been there for some time and the ground had become rock hard.

Stuart and Solo went on to find a number of weapons caches at Sorklehz near the Patrol Base. These were covered by rocks in small re-entrants. Solo located a brandnew PKM light machine gun with about 400 rounds of ammunition. An hour or so later Stuart and Solo found five RPG rounds plus four recoilless rifle rounds in a hidden Taliban ammunition cache. The team continued to find small caches in dry creek beds and in walls over the next few weeks.

On 25 February 2010, after more than nine months in-country, Stuart and Solo returned to Australia. Their return route was from Tarin Kowt to Dubai, then from there to Townsville where most of the EDD section departed on leave. The dogs completed their 30-day quarantine and veterinary checks in Sydney before being released back to 3 CER for more EDD duties.

3 CER Townsville

Once the dogs and the sappers returned to duty at 3 CER, continuation training resumed as the dogs needed to get back into the swing of things after their 30-day non-military vacation at Eastern Creek. Soon the EDD teams were training four days a week and ramping up for their operational assessments.

This training is frustrating for the EDD team trainers because it is based on Australian settings and does not replicate the conditions or scent pictures which are in Afghanistan. Stuart believes that the training situation should be reviewed with a focus on the current circumstances of the war in Afghanistan. The war is a dynamic entity with the enemy evolving new approaches and techniques to counter coalition troops. The intelligence which comes back from Afghanistan is not always being acted on as well as could be expected in respect of EDD training.

Stuart had an opportunity to volunteer for the Afghanistan

rotation in June 2011, but passed up the opportunity in favour of a Dog Training Supervisor Course at SME.

Corporal Cam Elliott, an SME EDD trainer and instructor, saw potential in Solo with his strong retrieval drive and quiet but cooperative nature. It did not take long for Cam to have Solo looking for explosives and he decided to recruit him. It was Solo's lucky day because he had some age on him and would not have been selected through the normal recruitment process. He was teamed up with Stuart at SME and the pair have stayed together until this current day.

10.

THE FUTURE
OF MILITARY
WORKING DOGS

The future looks bright for Australian military working dogs. There is no sign of any modern technology being developed any time soon that will be able to cost effectively detect an offender or particular odour day or night in various environments and do something about it via indication or physical action. If anything we have yet to see the full potential of MWD development. The MWD is one of the world's fastest land animals with 42 sharp teeth heading for the enemy like a guided missile. Who really needs to improve that?

In future the Australian military dog may look like a science fiction figure with advanced protective body armour, all-terrain boots, eye-protective goggles, attached optical vision and acoustic aids to allow the handler to see what the dog can. The dog could then be issued commands at a safe distance, given advanced supplements or medications to enhance its performance, even perhaps a breathing system enabling it to work in contaminated environments – or anything else our imaginations could conceive.

In recent wars MWDs were found not only in the front line but usually leading the front-line units. During the early years of security guard dog deployments around bases and facilities, MWD teams were regarded as secondary troops. However, MWD handlers today have evolved into efficient Infantry soldiers well versed in combat skills and with high fitness levels.

In the future one improvement to the MWD team may be to up-skill handlers to veterinary technicians to give an in-situ first aid response, similar to having a combat medic in a platoon for immediate treatment, giving the MWD a better chance of survival if injured. MWDs will in the future only become more valuable, not necessarily in cost but as an asset.

Dogs still strike fear into the hearts of many enemies and comfort their allies by raising morale. ADF operations at the time of writing and over the foreseeable future are in lands where populations fear dogs because of their cultural or religious beliefs. This gives our troops a distinct advantage. During the Gulf War the sheer presence of the dogs at military installations was a huge deterrent for would-be troublemakers, both because of their intimidating size and because this population were generally scared of the animals.

Dogs give future commanders search and force protection capacities and they also provide a vital extra level of search capability, whether they are looking for people, explosives or arms. Perhaps the future of MWDs lies in what they have done so successfully in the past. They are a cost-efficient way to patrol large areas that have to be protected. During the Vietnam war Da Nang was guarded by US Marines and hundreds of South Vietnamese troops and guard towers but not until MWDs were employed as perimeter patrol dogs did the constant raiding take a severe downturn. In prisoner-of-war situations one MWD can control many times its number by its deterrent value and physical presence. This was evident during the Gulf War when Royal Air Force dog handlers were responsible for guarding Iraqi prisoners. One dog team was often seen guarding thousands of enemy troops.

Although the sterling work of the MWDs and their handlers may have escaped much of the public eye in the media, they are recognised as operational gold dust by commanders and fellow troops in Afghanistan. Soldiers find it really comforting when the dogs go out with them leading from the front. Being on point is one of the most nerve-racking jobs of an Infantry soldier. When a recent survey was conducted with those serving on Operation Telic 10, the British name for the operational mission in Iraq, troops were asked: What pieces of kit had made the biggest difference on front-line operations? The humble dog received an extraordinary amount of votes. Should a future conflict, given all the climatic warnings we receive today, alter the concept or conflict zones by changing our current desert warfare trend into an Arctic warfare requirement, perhjaps skills such as sledge dog-hauling will once again be required. The last formal government experience Australia had in this field was with Antarctic scientific sledge dog teams, which ended when dogs were banned from the continent – the last left in 1993. As recently as 2010 the Royal Army Veterinary Corps (RAVC) sent members from its 104 MWD unit to Canada to enhance their skills in sledging and understand special requirements of working with dogs in Arctic environments.

Likewise the Military Police Dog (MPD) teams, during ongoing operations in East Timor and the Solomon Islands, have used skills their Vietnam predecessors perfected a generation before. One of these is the art of visual tracking; in Vietnam soldiers were taught the art of visual tracking to support canine tracker teams.

One such visual tracker and member of the ADFTWDA is Ian Hall. Corporal Ian 'Ben' Hall joined the Regular Army and graduated into the Royal Australian Infantry. He was 18 years old. He joined the fledgling B Company 6 RAR Anti-tank Platoon of Support Company 6 RAR. In May 1965, 6 RAR arrived in Tan Son Nhut airbase in Saigon. From Saigon 6 RAR went to various posts within Vietnam, ending up in Nui Dat. The Anti-tank Platoon became an additional rifle platoon for D Company as the local Viet Cong (VC) and North Vietnamese Army (NVA) units did not operate armour. A useful feature of the Anti-tank Platoon was that its members were also trained as reconnaissance soldiers. This set them up for their most useful employment as trackers who could use their recon skills to follow-up an enemy 'sign'. This included boot marks, cigarette butts and discrete enemy bush signals (for example, twigs shaped into mine markers). Ben was a member of 6 RAR when D Company 6 RAR clashed with the enemy in what has become the iconic battle for Australians in the Vietnam War, the battle of Long Tan. He arrived on the scene with the relief column after the main attacks had been defeated by D Company. Decisions taken after the battle of Long Tan was that the Anti-tank/Tracker/Recon Platoon should have a fully trained medic who could be called on when the platoon was acting independently on recon tasks. Ben was selected and doubled as the platoon medic right up until the time he returned to Australia.

Back in Australia Ben was promoted to lance corporal and then, in June 1968, to corporal. At about that time, Ben attended an Engineer demolition course and shortly afterwards the platoon went to the Tracker Wing at Bardia Barracks at Ingleburn to develop more knowledge of tracking and dogs. The course contained two elements, including visual tracking and tracker team employment. On his return to 6 RAR at Townsville, Ben became a tracker team leader. The platoon took on a more recon flavour and in May 1969, 6 RAR departed for its second tour of duty in Vietnam.

This time Ben and the trackers were located in the Support Company lines near the Battalion headquarters. On arrival, the platoon took over the dogs from 4 RAR/NZ (ANZAC Battalion) including Marcus, Milo and Trajan. Operation Lavarack was launched in which all tracker teams were deployed. They operated out of Fire Support Base (FSPB) Virginia with the purpose of locating and then following the tracks which led from a bunker system, recently occupied by the enemy. During this period, the trackers had contacts with VC soldiers and on each occasion tracking them down was the method of establishing enemy contact. Milo was instrumental in tracking two VC until contact was established. One VC was killed in action, the other disappeared. On 2 October 1969, two tracker dog teams were deployed into the Nui May Tao hills where a missing SAS soldier had fallen from a rope under a helicopter. He was Trooper G J. Fisher wo had been wounded during a hot extraction. He was not located but a contact resulted in one VC killed in action. In May 1970, 6 RAR/NZ completed its tour of duty and returned to Australia. Ben served the Queensland Police Service for 34 years, retiring in 2006 to a rural life. He has served as the ADFTWDA treasurer and merchandise manager with his partner and long-time ADFTWDA active supporter, Ann Dickenson.

With the concept of a hardened Army (better protected) within the ADF it makes sense to provide MWD teams, which on many occasions operate well into the front lines, with armoured protection in the form of their own specialist vehicle suited to dog requirements. In current operations, with a greater increase in roadside bombings and suicide incidents, the need for armoured protection has increased. Likewise, the terrorist modus operandi in current conflicts has shown that support and rear echelon forces are equally vulnerable to attack. MWDs worldwide are finding an increasing role in protecting facilities, VIPs and support structures because terrorists see these as weak and easy targets. Increasingly MWDs are placed in harm's way to protect them and must be likewise protected with armoured vehicles.

The current role of the MWD teams include searches at vehicle check points or deployment to conduct search and seizure operations well into hostile-held territory; these require better protection than soft-skin vehicles as transport. In many cases it appears the tradition of transporting a MWD team is to simply throw them in the back of an armoured vehicle with other troops heading in the same direction.

Very few countries have provided specialist canine vehicles with armoured protection. Yet in peacetime many police and military units do provide custom-built dog vehicles with ventilation, separation cages and storage facilities to house this vital asset. In fact many Australian state and federal laws as well as the animal welfare and humane societies require dogs to be transported in a safe manner. MWDs take a considerable time to train and therefore replace and are indeed a substantial fiscal investment to the military.

Dogs require air-conditioning and ventilation systems. It was shown that when hot, MWDs stationed in Iraq, where temperatures can soar up to 50 degrees Celcius, for example, tire quickly and their ability to detect explosives and other dangers was greatly reduced. The Army Combat Engineers have converted six Land Rovers into dog vehicles fitted with cages and they can transport all necessary stores. An ideal version in the ADF could be the conversion of a Bushmaster (ute type) into a specialist dog vehicle. This would provide mine protection for crew/handlers and MWDs in front-line operations.

Another future consideration in the ADF was illustrated in recent deployments by both the British and US forces in Iraq and Afghanistan, which showed the need for better cooperation and joint training between all services MWD units. This has been highlighted by several factors. Firstly, one of manpower: simply put, there are not enough MWDs or personnel within the US Army to cope with the mission objectives. Therefore, the US Army was required to supplement its MWD teams with counterparts from the USAF, Marines and Navy. Likewise in the British Forces, the Royal Air Force Police have had to fill major shortfalls within the British Defence capability by deploying alongside their Army counterparts.

In short, it's all about manpower and using the resources available to better fulfill the missions tasked to us. It's also important to ensure all MWD teams can perform core skills that are inter-changeable with all services, thus optimising manpower – this is a far better option than temporary recruitment increases in any one service to fill a mission requirement.

In Australia each service trains their own military working dogs, which might make sense if they each needed a specialty role for their separate modus operandi, but they don't. Military working dogs used in that role could all be trained at one centre – in this case the RAAF for all three branches. Explosive Detection Dogs are a mixed bag. The Army (the lead agency in this field) train their own EDD teams. The RAAF even contract out to the Customs Department for EDD training, despite the Army having experts in the field with current Afghanistan experience.

Recent deployments by ADF in Afghanistan have showed there are not enough EDD dogs or personnel within the Army to cope with the mission objectives. Many handlers and dogs are conducting multi tours of duty. In some cases both man and canine are showing signs of stress. This manifests itself in staff turnover. There is a need for better cooperation and joint training between the MWD units. Simply put, the RAAF EDDs should be able to supplement their EDD counterparts in the Army. The RAAF has over a dozen EDD teams fully trained in Australia but due to a mix of politics, fragile egos and suspicion, the green team will not play with the blue team. It is of course not as simple as that, RAAF handlers would require to upskill in combat tactics for their own safety and for the safety of the unit they are deployed with outside the wire.

In the ADF we have three dog training schools, one in the RAAF and two within the Army. I concede we will probably never get down to one dog school in the ADF, although I cannot see why not. The police forces within this country seem to be able to train both general-purpose police dogs and specialist dogs easily enough and in greater numbers in many cases than the Defence Force. A far more efficient system to start within the ADF would be for the RAAF to train all MWDs and the Army to train all EDDs. We should have a joint-service approach to training MWDs to ensure all MWD handlers can effectively work together in peace and war. The key is to ensure all MWD teams can perform core skills that are inter-changeable within all services, thus optimising manpower. This can be achieved by a combination of joint training and exercises, standard operating procedures and exchange of instructional staff. It is a far better option than temporary recruitment increases in any one service to fill a mission requirement.

Separate training can and does create scepticism over quality of training from one branch to the other, and this is not only unnecessary but unproductive. I must point out this is in no way at the sharp end of the job. All handlers from all services and civilian agencies get on very well and train and cooperate professionally. It appears to go pear shaped at higher command when someone wants or thinks he needs to protect his own little empire instead of looking at the bigger picture. Maybe it might help in the future if MWD teams were commanded by subject-matter experts who not only have an appreciation of core capabilities of MWDs but are not given other duties distracting their primary focus.

Another area of possible expansion in the MWD world is to look backwards as far as their welfare maybe concerned. Many will be surprised by the suggestion of re-establishing a corps within the ADF that bases its modus operandi on animals instead of advanced technology in the 21st century. The ADF Veterinary Corps was initially established between 1903 to 1946. Since that time the ADF has had no professional resources to deal with animal-related matters, even though we maintain numerous animals within the ADF.

From the Sudan Contingent, the South Africa war, WWI and through to the end of WWII, veterinarians provided professional care for horses and other animals of the Australian Army. There is no veterinary corps in today's Australian Army but in WWI half of the land transport needs were provided by horses, donkeys and mules. An Australian veterinary hospital established at Calais in 1917 was designed to accommodate 1250 animals and had an establishment of seven officers and 459 men of the Veterinary

Corps. A military information website states that eight million animals perished in the Great War. Veterinarians were much needed to care for the horses of the Australian Light Horse in the Middle East. Another charge for the vets was to maintain the camels used by Australians serving in the Imperial Camel Corps. A sad day for the Light Horsemen came when they were forced to leave their horses behind when they returned to Australia. Most horses were shot by their owners as they dreaded them falling into the hands of locals who they believed would work them to death.

During WWII, the old Light Horse units were mechanised and there was not so great a demand for the services of veterinarians as in previous wars. They were required in New Guinea, however, to service the Pack Transport Companies and Pack Batteries of the artillery used in inhospitable terrain. The few military dogs used in WWII were treated by them or Commonwealth vets.

The ADF currently operates in many conflicts or humanitarian theatres where terrain and populations rely on animals exclusively. An example of why and how it is important to retain animal skills within the ADF is outlined in the British Army veterinary specialist arm, the Royal Army Veterinary Corps (RAVC), job description.

The RAVC is a technical support Corps, small but competent. Deeply involved in all aspects of military animal activity and related matters, RAVC personnel enjoy a challenging and varied employment role involved in all aspects of the use of animals for military purposes, from their procurement, through their initial assessment and training, the maintenance of their health and fitness throughout their service life, to their retirement from the service. The RAVC are also involved in the welfare of Civilian animals during Operations and their rehabilitation post conflict.

These fundamental principles are as good today as at any future time and sit well with the present ADF military philosophy of cost-effectiveness, efficiency and operational preparedness.

The US Army Veterinary Service is an integral part of the Army Medical Department. It is composed of more than 700 veterinarians, 80 warrant officers, and 1800 enlisted soldiers in both the active duty and in the Army Reserves. The United States Army Vet Corps (USAVC) has been drastically increased over recent years to fulfill the requirements of supporting animals in countries they are currently deployed in. Such countries rely heavily on animal transportation systems and animals play a large part of the population's wealth, security and status. The USAVC have realised that after a major operation not only human but animal casualties affect a population because of the economic dependency. To win over local leaders and the general population, the USAVC ensure stock is replaced, animals are given medical treatment and transportation infrastructure (equine) is given top priority. In peace-time the US Army Veterinary Service is responsible for providing care to MWDs, ceremonial horses, working animals of many Department of Homeland Security organisations, pets owned by service members and animals supporting Human-Animal Bond (HAB) programs at military hospitals.

Within the ADF, the use of animals is on the increase as opposed to decline. This is primarily due to MWDs and EDDs being used to combat terrorist activities in both homeland defence and offensive operations. These units include the Engineers, Military Police and RAAF MWD teams.

It is not just dogs of course. In 2002 in Afghanistan, Australian SASR members at Bagram Air used equines to transport supplies, (their names: Simpson, Murphy, Roy and HG). Not your typical troopers but four grey donkeys. When the SASR joined the international forces to overthrow the Taliban regime, naturally they had all the latest military technology. However, they found donkeys not only helped them blend in with the surrounding landscape but in the mountainous terrain around Bagram donkeys are more practical to use than four-wheel-drive vehicles.

None of these ADF animals are governed by a professional veterinary body and veterinary services are currently supplied by various civilian contractors. There is no capacity to have veterinary services from these civilian contractors deployed to operational areas where MWD currently operate if the need arises.

An ADF veterinary corps could still provide a valuable function in training the forces of developing nations in the use of animals, such as equines, as viable transportation options. Equines still hold a place in many developing nations which the ADF may find itself supporting in the future. AVC members could further train local forces in the use of guard dogs. Members could also give expert advice on military animal-related issues such as farm animals and draft animals. During its initial years ADF AVC staff were trained in agricultural livestock awareness and husbandry to enable any local animal injured by friendly forces to be treated. Advice was also given in this area to assist local farmers in increasing livestock production. This goes a long way toward winning local hearts and minds.

Therefore, an Australian veterinary corps would have several functions:

1. To provide veterinary advice to the ADF via reserve vets, vet nurses and other specialists such as farriers.
2. To provide humane animal care in peace and war on operational missions (acting in a similar role to the RSPCA in active and post-conflict areas).

3. To support developing countries in an advisory role on animal welfare and animal management to local peoples on operational or humanitarian missions. This can include domestic and agricultural stock.
4. To have an element of animal trainers, such as equine and canine instructors/ advisors, in its ranks to aid the above missions.

Years of war and frequent deployments have affected military working dogs just as they have humans. In 2011 the USA appointed a specialist to treat post-traumatic stress. Dr Walter Burghardt the chief of behavioural medicine for military working dog studies, assigned to the Daniel E Holland Military Working Dog Hospital at Lackland Air Force Base. Burghardt stated:

> The dogs that go overseas are starting to show some distress-related issues. This includes hyper vigilance or showing interest in escaping or avoiding places in which they used to be comfortable. For example, a dog that used to work at a security checkpoint or gate may try to pull away on his leash when he sees he's being led to that checkpoint or gate. Some of the dogs also become very clingy or more irritable or aggressive.

Several of the older ADF EDDs are suffering from PTSD after several tours of Afghanistan. These have been returned to Australia.

Reserves
Reserves can offer a great deal to MWD programs. However, the RAAF maintains a very small number of reserve MWD handlers; the Military Police nil and the Combat Engineers used a few in a support not handling role.

The nature of dog handling in the military requires young, active personnel of a junior non-commissioned officer rank usually; thus, if a serviceman is career orientated very few vacancies above senior NCO exist for those personnel who wish to remain in the dog trade. No commissioned officer patrols or handles a MWD in the ADF. The result is that good experienced dog handlers have to either leave the physical handling of dogs or leave the service completely.

The overall outcome is that often good JNCOs (with great amounts of dog handling experience) are left waiting – as the phrase goes – for dead men's shoes to fill, and so leave the service for civilian equivalent jobs. The Australian Police, Corrective Services and Customs dog sections and private dog training schools are full of ex-ADF dog handlers.

In the future we need to expand the Military Reserve MWD handler program to retain this expertise. There are many jobs a reserve doggie can do, including instruction, kennel management, garrison patrolling and UN peacekeeping missions. One example of the need to retain reserves' knowledge is Corporal Jim Hoy. Jim served in the Regular Army as an EDD handler for many years conducting operations including in the Solomons. In 2008, as an Active Reserve (ARES). Jim temporarily rejoined the colours and conducted a tour of Afghanistan.

The day after Jim arrived back into Australia he was discharged again from full-time duty and allocated back to his ARES position in 2 CER, Brisbane. Jim went on post-combat duty leave and then resumed his job with Customs in the Maritime Unit. Six months later he was officially de-briefed and he became an Inactive Army Reservist. Jim would be happy to come back into the ARES in an EDD training role. He believes that there is plenty of scope for ARES employment in the EDD stream in areas such as rewrites of EDD training doctrine or providing on-the-job training for EDD trainees and training dogs.

Clearly, there is intellectual property available to the Australian Defence Force by encouraging combat-experienced personnel to take up Defence Reserve positions and pass their knowledge onto the current cohort of the Defence community. Jim could mix a position with Customs border protection dogs with an ARES contribution to the EDD stream. The winner in that mix of Jim's considerable experience, dedication to duty and knowledge would be the Commonwealth of Australia.

One thing is for sure, MWDs will be around for the future. Why? Maybe it's just because war dogs saves lives. Ask any Infantry soldier on point if the patrol want a MWD out in front and 100 per cent will say yes.

In July 2010, the then Minister of Defence, Senator John Faulkner, said, 'Australian forces in Afghanistan currently face a very high risk from both insurgent operations and improvised explosive devices, and a high risk from indirect fire.' The government's investment in force protection capabilities includes a range of measures to provide direct protection for Australian Defence Force members from small-arms, improvised explosive devices and indirect fire. These measures will include additional military dogs.

Current operations include EDD teams in Afghanistan and recently Military Police (MPD) operational deployments to Timor-Leste deploying a Fly Away Team. Both Military and Federal Police (AFP) deployed teams in an attempt to restore law and order in that country and in the Solomon Islands. Today Australia's combined military services use more MWDs than at any time in its history.

In the future it is important to not only retain MWD skills

but continue to improve their effectiveness in several ways – for example, training MWD handlers in visual tracking techniques and employing those skills to supplement the MWD will enhance the pursuit of the enemy wherever they are located, enabling an area to be dominated and reduce the activities of the enemy. Historically, the ability of employing visual trackers to locate and interdict a subject has been used by many militaries around the world with a great deal of success. The British Army has maintained a tracking capability based on their combat experiences during WWII, Malaysia, Kenya, Cyprus and Borneo. Today visual tracking is taught through their Jungle Warfare Wing in Brunei. The Malaysians have also retained a Visual Tracking School since the British moved their Jungle Warfare School to Brunei. The Australians and New Zealanders have recognised the value of tracking since 1942 when soldiers from both countries were trained in Australia by British instructors for the conduct of unconventional warfare operations behind Japanese lines during WWII. Today both countries still run tracking programs for their soldiers based upon the experiences and lessons learned from the Vietnam War where visual trackers supported combat tracker teams. Even recently the Fijian, New Zealand and Australian soldiers have conducted tracking patrols in conjunction with Australian Military Police dogs in East Timor.

As I explained in the introduction, the main reason I wanted to write this book was to bring to the attention of Australians that animals, in this case canines, have served the colours too. During the course of writing my attention has been brought to appeals from associations such as ADFTWDA and the RSPCA who contacted politicians in the hope that war dogs one day can be formally recognised by our own government. One politician replied that dogs could not get a medal because they didn't volunteer! They had no choice. This idiot has never heard of National Service or the fact that most armies in the world, including our own, draft people in times of war.

I do not think for one moment that a returned serviceman would be offended by a war dog getting a medal – it would not belittle his medal or his contribution but just recognise another digger's efforts, one with four legs not two.

K9 Combat Badge

One area which I believe needs attention is the issue of a canine combat badge for operational service. During the Vietnam War, for example, it was recognised that being on point in the Infantry on patrol in the jungle was one of the most dangerous of occupations. Some patrols were lucky enough to have scout dogs assigned to them. These handlers were not only in front they were way in front, not only of the squad but any point man or scout. Many of these handlers, however, did not qualify for the Infantry Combat Badge as they were on attachment from Engineer, Military Police or USAF Military Working Dog teams.

This same injustice is still happening today in places like Afghanistan, where MWD handlers, including members from the ADF, are leading patrols and Special Forces elements in the front line but are unable to claim the Infantry Combat Badge they so richly deserve.

Perhaps the ADF could look at the introduction of a combat engineer badge for the EDD handlers or a tri-service recognition for all MWD handlers during combat operations.

In the 1970s the British Army introduced the RED PAW badge which was issued to handlers serving as EDD handlers in Northern Ireland.

This is not about badge collecting – if you think that then get rid of all badge recognition. This is about the issue of a physical object that recognises the specialist and unique contributions dog handlers provide to the ADF.

Another aim is to remove dogs from the Army listings as a stores item, give them their own service numbers and recognise their special requirements as living beings. Finally, this book is not about war but to honour the warrior both handler and dog. It is my hope that one day animals will never be needed to fight alongside humans in war, and of course we all pray that people too never have to go to war. But if we do, man's best friend is ready to go with us.

11.

LEST WE FORGET

Australian has a long history in the use of animals in war since the country's founding. Today that focus is on military dogs as many organisations and individuals still battle for our canine comrades to be formally recognised by memorials or government-issued awards.

Sadly, our history has been slow to recognise animal contributions during war. Hundreds of thousands of horses left the shores of Australia in WWI and only one, Sandy, the mount of General Bridges, ever returned. Mules, the unsung heroes of the ADF, were used to transport millions of tons of supplies over the first and second world wars. More sure-footed than horses, they were used to pull artillery from the mud of the Somme and the jungle mountains of south-east Asia. Donkeys, which embodied the image of the ANZAC spirit based on the famous image of Simpson and his donkey Murphy rescuing wounded comrades, were used by the thousand. After both wars, many of these animals were left to the locals, with many being mistreated and worked to death. Military working dogs loaned to ADF units in previous wars were on the whole spared this fate because they were returned to the British or US Forces they came from. Sadly we've learnt nothing about respecting our four-legged fellow servicemen and in Vietnam many dogs were never returned home due to government quarantine policies. We can never let this happen again to our canine comrades in arms.

We are not the only country at fault, however. Sadly more dogs lost their lives after WWI than during it. An estimated 100,000 dogs served on all sides during WWI and tens of thousands were killed in the conflict; however, many armies simply destroyed their service dogs at war's end. The French destroyed all their 15,000 dogs.

The wearing of medals is an outward sign of the virtues against which soldiers are measured. For these distinguishing qualities, a soldier is given medals and the recognition of his country. Military working dogs also possess these qualities. Man's best friend has faithfully served the ADF in wars for many years as scouts, sentries, messengers, and much more. They have served in many conflicts without compensation or recognition, nor been honoured for their sacrifice. These gallant dogs have more than earned the right to be fully recognised for their service to their countries. Thankfully, this is starting to change.

Again we are not the only country to be slow off the mark. The US, one of the world's largest users, hasn't always shown its gratitude to service dogs. For nearly a century, an estimated 100,000 dogs have served in the US military, doing jobs in explosive and mine detection, tracking and scouting. Dogs have carried messages and stood watch as sentries. Early on, dogs were donated by the civilian population in order to fill military needs. Later they were specially bred for the job. Dogs have served all over Europe, Vietnam, Bosnia, Kosovo, and today, are serving in Afghanistan and Iraq. For decades, veteran dogs deemed too old to serve (ten years and older) were euthanised. Now that's starting to change, thanks to a law passed in 2000, which allows retired military dogs to be adopted by their current or former handlers, law enforcement agencies or individuals capable of caring for them. For many years there was no national memorial to recognise the profound contributions of war dogs to the US military. That has been corrected in recent years, largely through the efforts of various Vietnam dog handler associations.

In March 2010, the US House of Representatives approved a resolution introduced by Congressman Leonard Lance honouring military working dogs of America for their service. 'Throughout our nation's history military working dogs have made great contributions to help our military men and women accomplish their important missions,' Lance said during a speech on the House floor. 'These dogs have helped save lives and protect our soldiers in harm's way. For more than six decades military working dogs have helped prevent injuries and saved the lives of thousands of Americans'. We have yet to hear our Parliament utter similar words.

On a scale smaller than memorials, some units have devised medals to honour their combat hero dogs. In some cases these were officially sanctioned by governments or have been produced by the efforts of individuals or groups to honour their canine comrades.

The Dickin Medal was instituted in 1943 by Maria Dickin to honour the work of animals in war. It is a large bronze medallion, bearing the words 'For Gallantry' and 'We Also Serve' within a laurel wreath, carried on a ribbon of striped green, dark brown and pale blue. Traditionally, the medal is presented by the Lord Mayor of the City of London. It has become recognised as 'the animals' Victoria Cross'. Since its inception, it has been awarded 26 times to service dogs.

In 2009 some of Australia's unsung military heroes were finally recognised for their bravery. For the first time, unofficial medals have been awarded to the country's courageous canines by the Australian Defence Force Trackers and War Dogs Association. Six medals, two of them posthumous, were presented to EDD teams of 2 Combat Engineers Regiment at a ceremony at Brisbane's Army barracks. The 2 CER commanding officer, Lieutenant Colonel Joel Dooley, awarded the medals in a regimental parade near the 2 CER Regimental headquarters. He said 'This is a significant occasion recognising the service these dogs provide to the nation. Their service is a reflection of the dedication and professionalism demonstrated by the their handlers'.

In September 2007 three EDDs were killed on operations. During a patrol in Oruzgan province in southern Afghanistan, a Special Operations Task Group vehicle was hit by an improvised explosive device, wounding two soldiers. The wounds were assessed as slight, only requiring first-aid by their fellow soldiers, and they evacuated to a nearby ISAF hospital for further treatment. During a later route clearance task an EDD and his handler encountered a second improvised explosive device. The bomb detonated on discovery, resulting in the slight wounding of the handler and the death of the dog Razz. The handler continued with his duties. Razz was a veteran of the 2002 Commonwealth Heads of Government Meeting and the 2006 Melbourne Commonwealth Games. He joined Defence after beginning his career with Customs. Army spokesman Brigadier Nikolic said the actions of Razz and her fellow EDDs had saved lives. Improvised devices placed on public roads are designed to kill and maim people. Razz helped identify where the bomb was placed and sadly paid the ultimate price for her actions.' Her handler stated it was a huge bomb and poor Razz was vaporised. Razz not only saved his life but the lives of the troops around him. After the parade Razz's handler, Lance Corporal Turnbull, reflected on the times he had with Razz and said that she was part of his family. 'She was a wonderful dog. A top EDD that was very intelligent. She was a family member to me and I'll never forget her.'

In August 2007, EDD Merlin was tragically killed while on operations with RTF 2 nearing the end of the deployment. It was the second death of an EDD on operations. EDD Merlin began his life as Buster and lived his puppy years at the Sunshine Coast Animal Refuge Society on Sippy Creek Road, Tanawha. On a regular dog procurement drive, the 2 CER handlers tested Buster and, being happy with his retrieval drive, bought him, renamed him Merlin and sent him to SME to be enlisted and eventually taught the skills of an EDD.

Sapper Peter Lawlis stated, 'I always felt sorry for whichever soldier ended up being his handler. As it turned out, I was the only handler who had the pleasure of being his best mate.' Having just returned from the UK Exchange Program, Exercise Longlook, in October 2005, Sapper Lawlis was without a dog and the boys at SME decided to team him up with the newest of the new, Merlin. Peter wasn't disappointed as some handlers may have been, because he has always appreciated the underdog, and Merlin had that quality in spades. His very ugly appearance, but extremely loving and loyal nature, appealed to him so, quickly requalifying as a new dog team, they were both ready to get to work. And work they did!

On posting to 3 CER at the start of 2006, they began training for Operation Acolyte, support to the 2006 Commonwealth

Games in Melbourne. During the lead up to the Games, both Merlin and Sapper Lawlis had to work pretty hard, not just getting to know more about how each other operated, but also getting to know the boys of the regiment. Peter thinks they did all right, because the boys soon named Merlin 'Top Dog' on account of how handsome he was. They also learnt, however, that he could only be pushed so far, as sometimes his bite was actually worse than his bark – and his bark could be pretty bad.

After the Games were all over they were off again, this time to Timor-Leste as part of Operation Astute. In 2007 both Merlin and Sapper Peter Lawlis took part in predeployment training for RTF 2, allocated to 2 CER because their dog section had been disbanded. Once the lead-up training was over, Merlin and Peter deployed for the third time in two years, this time on Operation Slipper.

Merlin became a much-loved member of the deployment. From the Infantry guys in D Company 1 RAR, to the gentlemen of the Cavalry – both 2/14 LHR and B Sqn 3/4 Cav Regt – Merlin was known by all. Peter noted:

Merlin was a great friend over the two years we worked and lived together. When I had had enough he always listened to me sook it out. When it was cold out in the desert he always snuggled in and kept me warm. When the Dutch Artillery was firing overhead and Merlin was scared, I would hold him that little bit tighter to let him know he was all right. We looked after each other and it is with a heavy heart that I feel I let him down right at the end. He was a fantastically loyal and loving companion and I hope he can forgive me for dropping the ball right on the full-time siren.

EDD Andy, a two-year-old Kelpie-cross and a member of the Special Operations Task Group, was killed when struck by a vehicle within the Camp Holland complex at Tarin Kowt. Andy was laid to rest near the Camp Holland kennel complex alongside fellow fallen EDDs Merlin and Razz.

Another EDD called Aussie was awarded two medals for operational service and for his five years of service in the ADF. The eight-year-old golden retriever has served in Afghanistan and the Solomon Islands.

In 2010 Sapper Darrin Smith was killed at a roadside bomb incident in Afghanistan. Sapper Smith's military career commenced as part of the Army Reserve, enlisting 29 November 2001 and completing recruit training in January 2002, serving as part of 3rd Field Squadron, South Australia. Sapper Smith went on to complete his Combat Engineer suite of courses in 2004 and become part of the Regular Army, where he was posted to 1 CER Darwin in October 2004. While at 1 CER, he successfully completed his EDD handler course in December 2006.

Sapper Smith was posted to 2 CER in January 2009. His deployment as part of Mentoring Task Force 1 was his first operational deployment. He deployed in March 2010. As part of his tour he has been awarded the Australian Active Service Medal with Clasp International Campaign against Terrorism (ICAT), NATO Service Medal, and the Afghanistan Campaign Medal. Sapper Smith has also been awarded the Australian Defence Medal.

Sapper Smith's dog was Herbie, a three-and-a-half year old Collie cross. Sapper Darren Smith was killed in action at about 1100 hours Afghan time (1700 hours AEST) on Monday 7 June 2010. He was operating along a road with his EDD Herbie and Sapper Jacob Moerland, the three of them from 2 CER based in

Brisbane. A powerful roadside bomb was detonated by remote control when the three of them were about to conduct a check of the location of the bomb. Sapper Moerland and Herbie were killed instantly, and Sapper Smith was wounded. Sapper Smith tried to stand and help his mate and had to be forced back down to the ground in order for the medics to treat him. He was medivaced by helicopter to base hospital, but his wounds were so severe that shock and loss of blood took his life.

The president of the ADFTWDA, Lieutenant Colonel George Hulse (Retd) highlighted that the EDDs awarded do an exceptional job. These dogs are superbly trained, so are their handlers. We need to recognise their service and these medals from the Association are part of that recognition.'

The Peninsular Shire Animal Shelter (Redcliffe Region, Queensland) remembered Herbie as one of the dogs which they had released to Sapper Smith for training as an EDD. They mourn the loss of EDD Herbie, and all war dogs, and have commemorated this fact with a simple plaque dedication ceremony at the Animal Shelter in October 2010.

In the ADF, the Army also has MWD teams in the Royal Australian Corps of Military Police. Like their EDD counterparts from the Combat Engineer Regiment, the MPD has received medals for operational duties. Since the raising of the unit, four Military Police Dogs (MPDs) have made the ultimate sacrifice. In 2008 a simple service at the headquarters of the International Stabilization Force in Timor-Leste was held for the interment of MWD Ziggy. Ziggy was part of the MWD Fly Away Team stationed in Timor-Leste as an operational asset to assist with patrolling, tracking and apprehension duties when required in support of the infantry. Ziggy was teamed with Corporal Dean Jennings and died after being infected with viral meningitis. This was a sad time for the team because Ziggy only had a month to go on his deployment, before returning to Australia. Ziggy was cremated in Timor and his remains were interned in a memorial area after a service that was conducted by the Army chaplain. This was attended by a large majority of the battle group and the Joint Task Force. The memorial area has been created at the Australian Army HQ in Dili, beside two other MPDs that had died on earlier operations.

The ADFTWDA are issuing two medals:

1. The War Dog Operational Medal. This is issued to those military working dogs which have served for a minimum period of 28 days in a theatre of war or an area of operations.
2. The Canine Service Medal. This is issued to those working dogs which have served for a continuous period of five years.

The ADFTWDA has also awarded service dogs with medals from the Police, Corrective Services and other government agencies.

There are some heart-warming stories of Aussie service dogs that have been smuggled home. As more stories surface and international news channels pay tribute to heart-warming war-dog stories, hopefully more of these military mutts will find secure homes, post-service. It was not until late in 1993, following changes to government policy, that our war dogs were permitted to return to Australia. All those before this, including those that served in Vietnam, were left behind after the return of our soldiers. These were our 'mates' who served as valiantly as any soldier, and they, like any soldier, should not be forgotten.

There has been many a dog handler who has turned to his dog in the depths of war and told him things he would never say to another soldier. MWDs have been a source of friendship, family and true love to their handlers – the price they ask is just a pat and a smile. Military canines make contributions every day while they serve in our military. They are hard working and do a great job of saving the lives of their handlers and the troops who walk in their footsteps. While we often focus on the human cost of operations, we must never forget the ultimate sacrifice made by man's best friend.

This report from three MWD units, from November/December 2010, shows an example of the daily operational life and death of our four-legged comrades.

It is with great sadness that I am writing to you to let you know of the sad past few weeks we have had at RAAF Amberley Military Working Dog Operations Cell.

MWD Harry was euthanised on 5 Nov 10 due to old age and suspected bowel cancer. MWD Harry qualified as a MWD in Dec 02 and spent eight years with handler Corporal Tamara Hayward .

MWD Roxy was euthanised on 8 Nov 10 due to severe dental trauma. MWD Roxy qualified as a MWD in May 09, her handler was AC Bradley Frischkorn.

MWD Zico was euthanised on the 25 Nov 10 due to severe arthritis. MWD Zico qualified as a MWD in Mar 08, his handler was LAC Julian Dyer.

MWD Sye passed away on the 29 Nov 10 after suffering from Gastric Torsion, MWD Sye survived the operation; however, due to the stress on her heart and body sadly passed away after five days of treatment.

The following was received from Military Police Working Dog Section the same day.

> MPD Zac was laid to rest today after a long and distinguished service.
>
> It has been a difficult time for the Unit over the past month as they have 'lost' three of their four legged diggers.

In May 2011 the Military Police Dog section at Oakey established a cemetery for its four-legged comrades. It was blessed as sacred ground by the unit padre and had the first of several plaques placed on new headstones to recognise MWD dogs who have recently died. Many MP dogs have died or been killed in action in various locations, including Timor-Leste. With this new facility it is hoped a central point can be established to honour all canines that have fallen and will do so in the future. It is a simple cemetery as befits the simple yet loyal and unassuming service the MP dogs give. The event was well attended by civilian police dog handlers and members of the Australian War Dog Association.

Last Post

It is a very emotive subject to suggest which dog died in combat operations. Some have died directly from the enemies' hand, such as EDD Razz and Herbie. Others such as MPD Ziggy died from illness while on operations; another example occurred at RAAF Base Tenghah in Singapore as RAAF MWDs patrolled the tarmac area when the dog Hobo had an encounter with a snake, and although Hobo ate the cobra, he was bitten at least 16 times and died as a result of venomous poisoning. All have died during military service and should be honoured. Many, like my own MWD, have passed away peacefully at home in retirement after serving the colours for eight or so years. These deserve the recognition due to old diggers too.

I have given the dogs who served in Vietnam a special mention of their own as all were left there after the conflict. However, it is unknown how many dogs attached to, or used by Australian forces, in all wars prior to Vietnam died in conflict, let alone the whereabouts of their graves. The War Dog Memorial, which will be completed by 2012, situated within the RSPCA Headquarters at Wacol, Queensland, will give a focal point for them all.

One story that sums up the bond between a four-legged digger and his mate is the story of Lance Corporal Denis Ferguson, Royal Australian Infantry, and tracker dog Marcus. It shows the bureaucracy of the government and of officials who deal in facts not compassion when it comes to our animal soldiers. When he turned 17 in late 1965, Denis joined the Regular Army for three years. On graduation Denis was too young for overseas service and he was told that he needed to undertake further training courses. He applied for parachute and sniper courses but was unable to secure positions. Then a Corporal Arthur Eather approached him and asked if he liked dogs. When Denis said he did, the corporal took him to the Tracker Section and introduced him to the Tracker Dog instructional staff.

Denis commenced his tracker training and was allocated a dog named Marcus. The dog was donated by the then governor of New South Wales, His Excellency, Sir Roden Cutler VC. Denis and Sir Roden appeared on national television as part of a public relations exercise in support of Australian military forces. Denis teamed up with another dog handler, Private Peter Haran, and they became good mates. Peter had a dog named Caesar. Both teams trained hard in the Ingleburn/Holsworthy/Darkes Forest areas of New South Wales. It was hot work and the dogs and handlers were under constant pressure to perform. The trainers were always instructing the two handlers to 'read your dog' for alerts or prompts. Trails were provided by other soldiers and the dog teams would track them down. The 'fugitive diggers' would double back in a wide loop in order to ambush the dog teams, but this ruse did not work well once the handlers had experienced several of their dogs' pointing and alert behaviours. The training lasted for nine months and the dogs were also trained in discipline, no barking and living in the bush. At the end of the nine months training, Denis and Marcus, and Peter and Caesar were posted to the 2 RAR at Enoggera, Brisbane.

In quick succession, Denis and Peter attended advanced infantry training in 2 RAR, then battle efficiency training at the Jungle Training Centre at Canungra in Queensland, then they were off to the war in South Vietnam. In May 1967, Denis and Peter and their dogs became a part of the advance party of 2 RAR. The Nui Dat base was located in the province of Phouc Tuy and 1 ATF had responsibility to defend the entire province. Denis completed 13 months with 2 RAR at Nui Dat. When his tour of duty came to an end, in June 1968, he said farewell to Marcus and handed him over to Private Alvin Peterson without too much personal emotion because Marcus still had a lot of work left in him as a military tracker dog. In 1969, Denis's three-year engagement with the Army came up and he elected discharge. Denis worked in various jobs for about 12 months but found it too boring and he missed the camaraderie of Army life. He went to the recruiting office in Brisbane and signed up for another three years. After a short familiarisation course at the Infantry Centre in Ingleburn, he was posted to 2 RAR at Lavarack Barracks in Townsville. In May 1970, 2 RAR was deployed to Vietnam for its second tour of duty.

On arrival at Nui Dat a Land Rover picked Denis and his mates up, and took them to the Support Company lines, where he was shown his tent. It was exactly the same tent he had lived in three years previously. Even the same bed. Same chair, same table. His platoon sergeant took Denis to the dog kennels and said; 'That's your dog there.' Denis felt a huge wave of emotion go through him. It was Marcus. As Denis approached the kennels, Marcus was faced in the other direction and did not see Denis arrive. Denis had a special whistle he had used previously just for Marcus. Marcus heard the whistle and his head went up. Denis whistled again and Marcus spun around, saw Denis and bolted for him. The dog had tears running down its face. Denis had tears running down his face. Who says dogs can't cry? There were hugs and dog licks and the two mates were a tracker team again.

In 1971, Denis's tour of duty was up and he was to return home. Marcus was showing signs of ageing and Denis wanted the dog to come back to Australia with him. He requested permission and offered to pay the $700 quarantine costs to get Marcus home. But he was given a firm 'No!' The dog would stay in Vietnam. Denis was angry. He loaded a full magazine onto his rifle and approached the 2 RAR headquarters. But he was seen coming and the intent was transparent. He was ambushed by two Military Policemen who disarmed and apprehended him. He was immediately put on a helicopter which flew him to HMAS *Sydney*. One of the MPs said: 'Son, it's all over.' But it wasn't. The thought of abandoning Marcus haunts Denis to this day.

Perhaps the last word in this story of four-legged diggers should go to the former chief of defence, Air Chief Marshall A.G. Houston AC AFC, who stated:

We have received confirmation that Defence has endorsed 7 June to annually commemorate Military Working Dogs. The letter from the Chief of Defence in part reads: 'My staff have consulted with both Army and Air Force on this matter and I support the proposal …'

The importance of the MWD teams is recognised and highly valued by Defence. I endorse the selection of 7 June as an appropriate annual date to commemorate their contribution.

This has been another step in the formal recognition of the part played by our four-legged diggers. The Australian Defence Force Trackers and War Dogs Association (ADFT-WDA) organised the inaugural event, which was hosted by 2 AFDS. The event was attended by current, and former, handlers from RAAF, Army, Queensland Police, Queensland Department of Corrections, Customs, and representatives of the RSPCA. It is anticipated that Military Working Dogs Day will be celebrated each year into the future, on 7 June.

* * *

Most people are unaware that as well as the traditional commemorative red poppy, there is also a white poppy, symbolising peace, and a purple poppy, remembering animals that died during conflicts. The Australian War Animal Memorials issued the purple poppy to commemorate all the animal deeds and sacrifices in war. It can be worn alongside the traditional red one, as a reminder that both humans and animals have, and continue, to serve. Please wear a purple poppy and help raise awareness of these forgotten heroes.

I am a War Dog

High on a hill overlooking the sea,
Stands a statue to honour and glorify me.
Me and my mates that have all gone before,
To help and protect the men of the war.

I am a war dog, I receive no pay,
With my keen, sharp senses, I show the way.
Many of us come from far and around,
Some from death row, some from the pound.

I am a member of the canine pack,
Trained for combat and life on the track.
I serve overseas in those far off lands,
Me and my master working hand in hand.

I lift my head and look across the land,
Beside my master, I await his command.
Together we watch as we wait in the night,
If the enemy comes, we are ready to fight.

In the plantations of Nui Dat I do camp,
The smell print of the VC, to track, as I tramp.
'Seek 'em out boy!' my master does call,
Through the vines of the jungle, together we crawl.

I remember the day we were trapped underground,
With military wildfire exploding all around.
My master and I packin' death through the fight,
Comforting each other till the guns went quiet.
My master's tour of duty has come to an end,
Vietnam he will leave, I will lose a good friend.
No longer will we trudge through the jungles of war,
The canine, the digger, the memory will endure.

Now the years have passed and I patiently wait,
For God to receive me through His celestial gate.
Where I'll roam in comfort for ever more,
He'll keep me safe from the ravages of war.

Reproduced by kind permission Santina Lizzio

The Dogs of War

He was a dog of no account, a bastard breed someone threw out.
A Kelpie with a bit of Blue, perhaps some Border Collie too.
A dog endowed with working genes and sense of smell that's mighty keen.
The Army boys said, 'He will do, he's just the type we want it's true.
The work is hard, the terrain tough but we know this bloke's got the stuff.
He's got the stamina to work all day and this bloke will not shirk.'

So Herbie went to war as well. They relied on his sense of smell.
For Herbie's job was finding mines, thus saving those who walked behind
and on this day he found the trace; they saw it written on his face
but who would know the Taliban would detonate the mine by hand,
and Herbie's life came to an end along with his two mates and friends
before the mine could be disarmed – three mates were gone and others harmed

And Herbie's just one of a score of dogs that work – the dogs of war.
Each day bravely they lead the fray – with just a pat received in pay.
They give their all, their second chance. Time may be short, but just a glance
from one bloke in a uniform sets their tails wagging – Desert Storm.
Part of a team, the men rely – on canine smell and canine eye
and if perchance the canine dies – then men in uniform will cry.

So here's to Herbie, Hammer, Jack and and those that didn't make it back.
To those who served, and their lives gave – four-legged people, loyal and brave.
Who snuggled up when nights were cold – whose furry ears were often told
of the anguish and fear that dwelt within – they sympathised, men felt
the caress of a warm wet tongue, they listened when there was no one
but them to talk to in the night – when waiting for the call to fight.

He was a dog of no account, a bastard breed someone threw out.
Now Herbie's guarding heaven's gate – right alongside his human mates.

Maureen Clifford © 08/10

I Wait by the Gate

In a strange land I was sent, not knowing my fate,
In a pen I was put and I sat by the gate.
I watched and I wondered what do I do now?
Then I looked up and saw you, as you walked up and smiled.

We trained and we worked and I showed you my best,
You rewarded me and patted me and I did the rest.
Through tracks and paths and roads we did go,
And I was to smell, for traps that would blow.

Many times I stopped you from ending your life,
From an enemy trip wire, that was set to cause strife.
Never had I thought that we would ever part,
Because of the love, that we had in our hearts.
Oh, I was proud to walk by your side,
With all of your friends and being your guide.

Then one day you put me back in my pen,
You smiled, you patted me, and said 'Goodbye my friend.'
You looked back one more time,
And I saw the tears in your eye,
And I knew it was the last, your way of saying goodbye.

My life, it so changed when you went back home,
And I stayed behind to a fate still unknown.
It's been over 40 years since I've seen your face,
But I never forgot you, my friend and my mate.
So please don't worry, I'm waiting by heaven's gate,
For my best friend, my brother, but mainly my mate!

Reproduced by kind permission Ronald (Connie) Chronister

BIBLIOGRAPHY

Periodicals and Articles
Australian Working Dog magazine
Australian & NZ Defender magazine

Internet and Other Sources
www.anzacday.org.au/history/vietnam/dogs.html
http://home.iprimus.com.au/buckomp/
    RAAFPoliceHistory.htm
www.militaryworkingdogs.com/
http://aussietrackers.tripod.com/main-index.html
www.defence.gov.au/media/download/2009/
    Mar/20090306/index.htm
www.defence.gov.au/Army/RAE/docs/Sapper_2008.pdf
http://xk9.customer.netspace.net.au/history_raafpdogs.
    html

Individual Consultants

Major Adam Riley, OC SEW SME

Warrant Officer Aaron Barnett, RACMP

Sergeant David Skeels, EDD RAAF

Sergeant Shane Campbell MWD RAAF

Warrant Officer Squizzy Taylor, RACMP

Sapper Shawn Ward, 2 CER

Jim Hoy

Seamus Dohnerty

John Quane, Secretary, Australian Defence Force Tracker and War Dog Association

George Hulse, President, Australian Defence Force Tracker and War Dog Association

Ian Ben Hall, Australian Defence Force Tracker and War Dog Association

Anne McConnell, Australian Defence Force Tracker and War Dog Association

Bob Bettany, Australian Defence Force Tracker and War Dog Association

Peter Haren, author

Simone Heyer, Australian Defence Force

Stephen Dent, Australian Defence Force

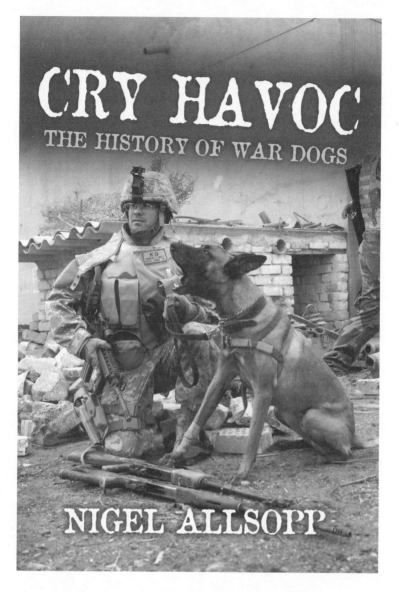

CRY HAVOC
THE HISTORY OF WAR DOGS

NIGEL ALLSOPP

From Babylonian war dogs with spiked collars to modern explosive detection dogs, canines have long been a soldier's best friend. Nigel Allsopp's *Cry Havoc* is the most authoritative and comprehensive book on the history of military dogs.